USING YOUR *Sunbeam* MULTI-COOKER FRYPAN

1. **PLUG IN**. Plug probe of heat control unit firmly into outlet with dial set on "OFF" position. Then plug cord into 120 volt AC wall or base electrical outlet.

2. **HEAT CONTROL**. To set temperature control to temperature recommended in recipe or on heat control rotate dial until recommended temperature is in line with point of arrow on control. The indicator light will go on. When it goes off, proper cooking temperature has been reached. Light will continue to go on and off during cooking indicating the temperature is being regulated.

3. **PREPARING TO COOK**. Preheat frypan, if recommended in recipe, before adding foods or recommended amount of shortening. When very small amounts of shortening are being used, tilt frypan slightly to coat entire surface. Fry or cook food as directed in recipes.

Time and temperature is approximate and will vary to suit taste, size and quantity of food. Foods taken directly from refrigerator to cook or fry will take longer than foods at room temperature, or a small quantity may require a lower temperature setting.

4. **SIMMERING**. To simmer in braising or stewing, the dial should be set approximately under the letter "E" in "SIMMER" which is about 220°. There will be a variation dependent on altitude. Do this simple test to find the simmering point of your frypan. Put 6 cups cold water into the cold frypan. Set dial at 260°. Do not cover. When water boils steadily, turn dial slowly back just to the point where the light goes off. This will be the approximate simmering point of your frypan. Set the dial at this point each time for simmering action. This will keep liquid gently bubbling when light is on. The signal light will flash on and off frequently.

5. **USE OF COVER**. Pan broiling, frying, sauteing and toasting sandwiches are generally done without the cover, unless indicated in recipes. Close vent on cover when moist heat is desired in cooking, such as in braising, stewing, etc. Open the vent when dry heat is needed as in roasting tender cuts of meat, finishing fried chicken, breaded chops, etc.

IF YOU HAVE A SUNBEAM BROILER COVER FRYPAN REFER TO SPECIAL INSTRUCTIONS AND RECIPES FOR BROILING ONLY.

Covered by one or more of the following patents: U. S. PAT. D-195,268; D-196,316; D-205,150; D-206,389; 3,068,342; 3,196,253; 3,218,434; 3,081,395   CONTINUED NEXT PAGE

6. **COMPLETED COOKING**. When food is fried or cooked as desired, set heat control at "OFF" position or in warm setting for serving or keeping foods warm. Serve directly from frypan if desired.

7. **UNPLUG**. To disconnect frypan, turn temperature control dial to "OFF" position. Remove electric cord of heat control unit FIRST FROM WALL OUTLET, then from frypan.

8. **SERVING**. Use unit for buffet or table service, setting dial at desired temperature.

CLEANING DIRECTIONS

1. To disconnect frypan, turn temperature control dial to "OFF" position. Remove electric cord of heat control unit first from wall outlet, then from frypan.

2. Wipe heat control unit with a damp cloth and dry, but do not ever put into water or any other liquid, or wash frypan while still connected.

3. Also, dry outlet area within shield prior to inserting probe, if used again immediately after washing.

4. Frypan is immersible in hot sudsy water for quick, easy washing. Let frypan stand until cool enough to handle. DO NOT IMMERSE FRYPAN IN WATER WHEN FRYPAN IS STILL HOT. Always carefully disconnect electrical cord before cleaning frypan.

5. Rinse in clean hot water and dry thoroughly as soon after washing as possible.

6. Certain strong alkaline detergents or very hard water may tend to darken the metal of your frypan. Cooking highly acid foods, such as tomatoes, sauerkraut, etc. tend to cause pitting of the metal surfaces. Remove such residue at once and rinse thoroughly.

7. On pans without "no-stick" cooking surface, steel wool scouring soap pads may be used LIGHTLY to remove particles clinging to the bottom of the pan. Do not scrape with sharp objects.

8. DO NOT STORE IN OVEN or ever put in oven because oven heat will damage plastic parts of handle and control unit.

NO-STICK COOKING SURFACE

IF YOUR SUNBEAM FRYPAN HAS THE "NO-STICK COOKING SURFACE" READ THESE USE AND CARE INSTRUCTIONS CAREFULLY

The no-stick, no-scour cooking surfaces may be used with metal cooking tools. Of course, reasonable care should be exercised in their use. Try to avoid digging into the finish or cutting into the surface with a sharp knife.

It should be pointed out that light or fine scratches on the no-stick surface seldom affect its non-stick properties. Such damage is really a matter of appearance and not performance.

1. Conditioning the surface (or seasoning the new frypan) — Before using your frypan for the first time, wash it with warm soapy water and a soft sponge or dishcloth. Be certain that it is oiled prior to the first use in order to condition the non-stick surface. This may be done by wiping the surface with salad oil.

2. Additional greasing — Generally speaking, it is not necessary to grease the no-stick cooking surface in order to prevent food from sticking. Most women find, however, that oils, fats, and butter are desirable in cooking because they add to the flavor of the food and also aid in even browning.

3. Cooking — Basically, the same procedures should be used for cooking with a frypan coated with non-stick properties as a frypan without this finish. Preheat your frypan, if recommended in fry guide or recipe, before adding foods. Add food and fry at temperature directed in recipes. If cooking oil is used, heat and add cooking oil, then add food. Avoid extreme temperature changes such as running cold water into a very hot frypan. Allow frypan to cool before soaking or rinsing after cooking. Grease and flour frypan when baking cakes directly in the bottom of the pan.

4. Cleaning — No-stick cooking surface frypans are extremely easy to clean and enable you to avoid long soaking time and tiresome scouring. Best results are obtained by following some simple rules:

(a) Always wash the pan in hot, sudsy water. Although water from the faucet will rinse away most visible residues, a thin layer of food or grease may cling to the surface and eventually build up and cause the finish to stain or even lose its release properties.

(b) Weekly scrubbing with a plastic or rubber scrubber or stiff sponge, to insure removal of grease or food residue is suggested to maintain highest level of release property.

(c) DO NOT USE STEEL WOOL, CLEANSER OR METAL SCOURING PADS ON THE NO-STICK COOKING SURFACE AS THEY WILL DAMAGE THE NO-STICK PROPERTIES OF THE SURFACE.

5. Removing stains from the finish — In time, the no-stick cooking surface will stain with continued use. This is considered normal and, within limits, does not affect the performance of the appliance.

While it is not possible to completely remove all stains, considerable success may be obtained with the Sunbeam Appliance Service Company Cleaner For No-Stick Finishes, available in leading food, hardware, appliance and department stores everywhere, as well as in Sunbeam Appliance Service Company stations throughout the United States. Then recondition appliance as instructed in step 1.

IMPORTANT PRECAUTIONS

1. After removing heat control from frypan, you may immerse the frypan completely in water. DO NOT HOWEVER IMMERSE FRYPAN IN WATER WHEN IT IS STILL HOT. Always carefully disconnect electric cord before cleaning frypan.

2. Do not use scouring pad on no-stick cooking surface.

3. Do not store unit in oven as this may damage plastic parts of handle and control unit.

4. Plug probe of heat control into unit BEFORE plugging other end into outlet. Be certain dial is set on "OFF" position.

SUGGESTIONS FOR GOOD RESULTS WITH FRIED FOODS

1. Use any type of shortening in preheated Frypan, such as vegetable shortening, salad oil, lard, bacon drippings, butter, margarine, etc. Melt before adding food. Use sufficient shortening to keep foods from sticking to bottom of pan.

2. Follow time and temperature indicated in recipe, varying to suit your taste, size and quantity of foods.

3. Avoid overcrowding foods when browning. When frying large quantities of chicken, etc., brown pieces without overcrowding. Remove to tray or plate while browning remaining pieces. Wait for indicator light to go "off" before browning another batch. When all pieces have been browned, return entire quantity to the Frypan and cover to finish.

4. Breading particles which adhere to the bottom of the Frypan may be removed with a wooden spoon or plastic spatula.

5. Keep paper toweling handy for draining fried foods such as bacon, sausages, etc. Bring the Frypan right to the table or buffet to keep foods piping hot. Makes most attractive serving unit.

6. After cooking or frying for time indicated, test for doneness with skewer or single tine of fork. Foods should be brown and cooked through well.

7. Foods such as chicken, chops, croquettes, etc., may be coated with any of the following: seasoned flour, beaten egg diluted with milk or water and fine dry crumbs, cornmeal or crushed cereals. Breading gives food a crisp, brown crust and moist interior with less shortening absorbed into the food.

SUGGESTIONS FOR COOKING FROZEN MEAT

Now meats can be cooked starting from the frozen state without any loss of flavor, only additional cooking time is necessary. The cooking methods remain the same as fresh or completely thawed meats.

ROASTS

When starting from the frozen state a small roast (2 to 5 lbs.) will require approximately ⅓ again the additional cooking time of a fresh roast. Midway through the cooking time turn roast, season and for the best results insert a meat thermometer.

STEAKS AND CHOPS

A hot Frypan is necessary for pan broiling steaks and chops. Why? To brown the meat before it has a chance to defrost on the surface and "water" in the Frypan. After browning, reduce the temperature and turn occasionally so the meat will cook through. A little fat can be added for better browning. The cooking time for frozen steaks and chops is ¼ to ½ again the required time for fresh meats.

LESS TENDER CUTS

Meats that are to be simmered may be browned in the frozen state in a small amount of fat and cooked slowly until tender. The cooking time required is about the same as fresh meat.

COMMERCIALLY

Frozen meat products should be prepared according to the package directions.

When browning frozen meats, set cover ajar on Frypan to prevent spattering.

SUNBEAM FRY-GUIDE

Many of the foods listed on this chart are also indicated on the Fry-Guide on frypan.

FOOD	Temperature	Approximate Frying Time	INSTRUCTIONS
BACON	340°	5-8 min.	Do not preheat. Arrange bacon slices in frypan. Avoid over-crowding. Fry, turning occasionally, until crisp as desired. Pour off fat during frying for very crisp results. Drain on paper toweling. Serve hot. (Half pound of bacon can be put in at one time. As bacon heats, slices can be quickly separated.)
EGGS (Fried)	300° 320°	2-4 min. 2-3 min. (For more crisp crust)	Preheat until light goes out, add 1 tbsp. or more of any de-sired fat for each 2 eggs. Melt. Add eggs. Spoon fat over eggs or cover. Fry until done as desired. Remove with pancake turner. Season. Serve with bacon, sausages or ham, if desired.
EGGS (Scrambled)	320°	1-3 min.	Beat together with a fork until blended—4 eggs, ¼ tsp. salt, dash of pepper, ⅓ cup milk. Preheat frypan until light goes out, add 2 to 3 tbsp. butter or margarine. Tilt so that entire bottom and lower sides are greased. Add eggs. Scrape slowly from bottom and sides with a spoon until set as desired. Sprinkle with paprika or finely chopped parsley.
PANCAKES	380°	2-3 min.	Use packaged mix recipe. Preheat until light goes out. Brush frypan lightly with fat or bake without greasing. (If batter contains no shortening, then grease.) Pour about 2 tbsp. batter for each cake, spacing a little apart. Bake until bubbly and puffed, then turn and brown other side. Serve at once or keep hot between folds of towel in a warm oven.
HAMBURGERS	360°	Rare 4-5 min. Well Done 6-10 min.	Mix together lightly with a fork—1½ lbs. ground beef, 1½ tsps. salt, 1 to 2 tbsps. grated onion (optional). Shape loose-ly into 6 patties about ½ inch thick. Wrap a slice of bacon around each, fasten with a toothpick (optional). Preheat frypan until light goes out, add 2 tbsp. fat. When melted, brown patties on each side. For medium or well done, turn dial to 300°. Continue frying and turning. Serve with sauteed mushrooms or onions.
HAM (Slices)	340°	10-20 min.	Use uncooked mild cure smoked ham cut ¼″ to ¾″ thick. Cut fat edge in several places. Preheat frypan until light goes out, add 1 tbsp. fat, melt, add ham, fry until well browned on each side and tender. When browned, tempera-ture may be set at about 220° and top of ham spread with 1½ tbsp. prepared mustard, ¼ cup brown sugar. Sprinkle with powdered cloves. Slowly add ½ cup gingerale, cover, simmer 10 min.
POTATOES (Country-fried) (Crispy Brown)	320° 340°	10-12 min. 10-12 min.	Slice thin, peeled, cold, boiled white potatoes. Add minced onion, if you like. Preheat frypan, add 2 to 3 tbsp. butter or fat, melt, add potatoes, fry without stirring until underside is brown. Turn, brown other side. Season with salt and pep-per. For Hashed Brown—combine 3 cups chopped cooked potatoes, 3 tbsp. flour, 1 tbsp. grated onion, ¼ cup top milk, 1 tsp. salt, ⅛ tsp. pepper. Preheat, add 3 tbsp. fat. Pack potatoes in firmly, spreading to cover bottom. Brown at 300° for about 15 min. Fold half over like omelet. Serve at once.
SAUSAGE	300°	12-15 min.	Do not preheat. Use link, country style or meat. Fry until golden brown and no pink color remains. Do not fry until dry. Turn frequently using tongs or two forks, so as not to break skins. Pour off excess fat. Saute apple or pineapple slices in sausage fat to serve as garnish. Brown precooked such as "Brown and Serve" for temperature and time di-rected on label.

FOOD	Temperature	Approximate Frying Time	INSTRUCTIONS
FISH	380°	5-8 min.	Use fresh or packaged frozen fillets, steaks or small whole fish. Thaw frozen fish, cut as desired. Dip fish in cold water or milk, then in mixture of ½ cup flour, ½ cup cornmeal, 1 tbsp. salt, ¼ tsp. pepper or dip first in well seasoned flour, then in mixture of 2 eggs beaten with ⅓ cup milk or water, then in fine, dry bread or cracker crumbs. Preheat frypan, add ¼ to ½ cup fat or salad oil. Add fish, fry until golden brown on underside, turn with pancake turner, brown other side. Fry only until easily flaked with a fork and still moist. Serve at once garnished with lemon pieces and parsley or a sauce.
PORK CHOPS (Breaded)	360° (brown) 220° (finish)	10-15 min. 30-40 min.	Trim off excess fat using scissors, cut small, add to frypan while preheating or use other fat. Snip fat edge of ½ to 1 inch thick chops. Sprinkle with salt, pepper, poultry seasoning. Dip into beaten egg diluted with 2 tbsp. water, then into fine dry crumbs, coating well. Brown well on each side —about 15 minutes. Add ¼ cup water and chopped onion (optional). When boiling, set dial at about 220°. Cover, open vent, simmer 30-40 min. longer or until no trace of pink remains (cut a slit near bone to test) and chops are tender.
CUBE or MINUTE STEAK	420°	2-4 min.	Have steaks flattened to about ¼" thickness. Preheat frypan until light goes out. Add 1 to 2 tbsp. fat. When very hot, add steaks. Do not crowd. Pan-broil 1 to 2 min. on each side or to desired doneness. Season. For pan gravy, add small amount hot water to drippings. Stir and heat, pour over steaks, Serve with sauteed onions, mushrooms or any desired sauce.
LIVER (Calf's, lamb, or tender beef)	360°	4-6 min.	Wipe ¼" to ½" thick slices with damp cloth. Cut out tubes with scissors. Dip liver in milk or buttermilk, then in well-seasoned flour. Preheat frypan, add 2-3 tbsp. fat or fry bacon first and use drippings. Brown liver quickly on each side. For well done result, turn dial to 240°, continue frying and turning. Serve with sauteed onions or bacon.
FRENCH TOAST	360°	2-3 min.	Beat together with fork until blended, 2 eggs, ¼ tsp. salt, 1 tbsp. sugar, ½ cup milk, ¼ tsp. nutmeg or ½ tsp. vanilla (optional). Preheat frypan, add 2 tbsp. butter or margarine, tilt to grease entire bottom. Dip slices of bread into egg mixture, only until coated. Fry at once until browned on both sides. Serve hot with syrup or applesauce. Fry full pan or dark bread at 380°.
CHICKEN (2 to 3 lbs.) CRUSTY CHICKEN (Use 4 cups fat.) Do not add water	360° (brown) 260° (finish) 400° (brown) 300° (finish)	12-15 min. 20-30 min. 12-18 min. 10-15 min.	Use clean market dressed chicken, cut in pieces. If frozen thaw first. Combine in paper bag, 1 cup flour, 1½ tsp. salt, ⅛ tsp. pepper, ¼ tsp. poultry seasoning. Drop few pieces at a time into this, shake bag until pieces are coated. Preheat frypan, add ½ cup shortening, oil or part butter and shortening, melt. Start browning meaty pieces first, putting less meaty pieces in between. Turn as necessary with tongs or two spoons. Fry until brown and crisp on both sides (12-15 min.) Set dial at about 260°, continue frying 20-30 min. longer or until tender. For less crisp, very tender chicken, set dial at about 230°, add ½ cup water, 1 chopped onion (optional). Cover, open vent, simmer 30 min. longer. Make cream gravy with drippings and some of remaining flour mixture.

GUARANTEE: Your Sunbeam Frypan is guaranteed for one year against electrical and mechanical defects in material and workmanship. Repairs or parts replacement required as a result of such defects will be made free of charge during this period. The guarantee does not cover damage caused by misuse, negligence, or use on current or voltage other than that stamped on the product. This guarantee is·in lieu of any other warranty, either expressed or implied. If service is required, send the product prepaid to the nearest Sunbeam Appliance Service Company station. Please write a letter explaining the nature of your difficulty.

SUNBEAM APPLIANCE COMPANY, a division of Sunbeam Corporation
5400 West Roosevelt Road, Chicago, Illinois 60650

HOW TO GET QUICK SERVICE:

1. Pack appliance carefully in a good carton with plenty of newspaper or excelsior padding all around it, and tie securely. Damage in transit is not covered by the guarantee.
2. Carefully print on the carton the name and address of the service station nearest you. Don't forget your return address.
3. Put a letter showing service desired in an envelope addressed to the same service station. In your letter please be sure to give full information; such as, date and place of purchase, your full name and address, and the service, or repairs, desired.
4. PASTE ENVELOPE TO PACKAGE.
5. Put First Class stamp on envelope, and Parcel Post stamps on package; then mail. (The Post Office will tell you the proper amount of postage and insure you against loss in the mails.)
6. Of course, if there is a service station in your community, you may take your appliance there in person.

SERVICE: **SUNBEAM APPLIANCE SERVICE COMPANY (SASCO)** is a subsidiary of Sunbeam Corporation specializing in servicing and repairing Sunbeam products. It has stations in many principal cities located throughout the United States as indicated below. Each station has a full stock of factory parts and is staffed by repairmen trained by factory methods.

Alabama
Birmingham 35222, 3615 - 5th Ave., South
Mobile 36606, 108 S. Florida Street

Arizona
Phoenix 85006, 1612 N. 16th Street

California
Fresno 93701, 1117 Belmont Avenue
Long Beach 90806, 2258 Pacific Avenue
Los Angeles 90017, 1238 W. 8th Street
North Hollywood 91601, 11154 McCormick
Oakland 94611, 2810 Broadway
Pasadena 91107, 2265 E. Foothill Blvd.
Sacramento 95814, 1924 T Street
San Diego 92104, 4028 - 30th Street
San Francisco 94105, 655 Mission Street
Santa Ana 92706, 816 W. 17th Street
Santa Clara 95050, 2100 De La Cruz Blvd.

Colorado
Denver 80204, 405 Federal Blvd.

Connecticut
Hartford 06114, 461 Wethersfield Ave.

Delaware
Wilmington 19801, 10 W. 4th Street

District of Columbia
Washington 20009,
1835 Columbia Road, N.W.

Florida
Hialeah 33010, 925 Hialeah Drive
Jacksonville 32207, 1636 Hendricks Ave.
Tampa 33609, 3424 W. Kennedy Blvd.

Georgia
Atlanta 30303, 276 Pryor Street, S.W.

Illinois
Chicago 60650, 5430 Roosevelt Road
Chicago 60602, 10 N. Clark St. - Suite 200
Chicago 60629, 3140 W. 59th Street
Chicago 60613, 3906 N. Lincoln Ave.
Chicago 60643, 11113 S. Western Ave.
Chicago, 60645,
Lincoln Village Shopping Center
6191 N. Lincoln Ave.
Downers Grove 60515, 1644 W. Ogden Ave.
Mt. Prospect 60056, 208 E. Rand Road
Niles 60648, 7639 N. Milwaukee Ave.
Peoria 61602, 833 Main Street
Rockford 61103, 3106 N. Rockton Ave.

Indiana
Fort Wayne 46807, 2710 S. Calhoun St.
Hammond 46320, 6347 Indianapolis Blvd.
Indianapolis 46202, 705 E. Market Street

Iowa
Davenport 52802, 1466 W. 4th Street
Des Moines 50314, 1477 Keosauqua Way

Kansas
Wichita 67202, 333 N. Waco Avenue

Kentucky
Louisville 40213, 3215 Preston Highway

Louisiana
New Orleans 70113, 807 Howard Avenue

Maine
Portland 04102, 263 St. John Street

Maryland
Baltimore 21201, 224 N. Paca Street
Beltsville 20705, 5020 Herzel Place
Langley Park 20783, 1333 Holton Lane

Massachusetts
Boston 02134, 1168 Commonwealth Ave.

Michigan
Detroit 48227, 15860 Schaefer Highway
Flint 48504, 4814 Clio Road
Grand Rapids 49504, 1050 Scribner, N.W.

Minnesota
Minneapolis 55408, 404 West Lake Street

Missouri
Kansas City 64111, 3120 Terrace Street
St. Louis 63103, 3442 Lindell Blvd.
360 S. Independence Blvd.

Nebraska
Omaha 68114, 7561 Dodge Street

New Jersey
Little Ferry 07648, 315 Route 46
Montclair 07042, 223 Glenridge Ave.
Newark 07108, 54 Elizabeth Ave.
Paterson 07505, 126 Broadway
Ridgewood 07451, 47-49 Hudson Street

New York
Albany 12205, 1555 Central Avenue
Brooklyn 11201, 27 Smith Street
Buffalo 14203, 1006 Main Street
Carle Pl., L. I. 11514, 245 Westbury St.
Elmsford 10523, 272 Main St. - Rt. 119
Flushing 11355, 136-17 41st Avenue
Little Neck 11362,
245-18 Horace Harding Expy.
New York City 10001, 128 W. 31st Street
New York City 10017, 21 E. 41st Street
Rochester 14609, 1099 E. Main Street
Syracuse 13202, 610 S. Salina Street

North Carolina
Charlotte 28204,

Ohio
Akron 44308, 319 Water Street
Cincinnati 45202, 550 Reading Road

Cleveland 44114, 1736 St. Clair Ave., N.E.
Columbus 43215, 111 E. Long Street
Dayton 45420, 704 Watervliet Ave.
Toledo 43613, 2364 Sylvania Avenue
Youngstown 44507, 3405 Market Street

Oklahoma
Oklahoma City 73107,
538 N. Pennsylvania Avenue
Tulsa 74120, 1410 E. 6th Street

Oregon
Portland 97232, 3203 N. E. Sandy Blvd.

Pennsylvania
Allentown 18102, 1126 Linden Street
Harrisburg 17101, 334 Chestnut Street
Kingston 18704, 429 Market Street
Philadelphia 19149, 2020 Levick Street
Philadelphia 19107, 117 S. 13th Street
Pittsburgh 15222, 1629 Penn Avenue
Upper Darby 19082, 40 Garrett Road

Rhode Island
Providence 02907, 320 Broad Street

South Carolina
Columbia 29201, 2608 Main Street

Tennessee
Knoxville 37917, 2411 Broadway, N.E.
Memphis 38104, 1701 Poplar Avenue
Nashville 37203, 1519 Church Street

Texas
Amarillo 79109, 2216 Canyon Drive
Dallas 75207, 2835 Irving Blvd.
El Paso 79903, 2908 Tularosa Street
Ft. Worth 76107, 3813 Camp Bowie Blvd.
Houston 77004, 4830 Almeda Road
San Antonio 78216, 7065 San Pedro Ave.

Utah
Salt Lake City 84110, 46 W. 4th South St.

Virginia
Falls Church 22046, 1071 W. Broad St.
Norfolk 23502, 4554 E. Princess Anne Rd.
Richmond 23230, 1921 Westmoreland St.

Washington
Seattle 98109, 411 Westlake Ave., North
Spokane 99201, 1514 N. Monroe Street
Tacoma 98402, 2511 S. Tacoma Avenue

West Virginia
Huntington 25701, 1036 - 3rd Avenue

Wisconsin
Green Bay 54303, 818 Lambeau Road
Milwaukee 53215, 3014 S. 13th Street

PORTABLE ELECTRIC COOKERY

by Bonnie Brown

A Benjamin Company/Rutledge Book

CONTENTS

Appealing Appetizers   7

Superb Soups   15

Magic with Meats   23

Perfect Poultry   47

Fabulous Fish   61

Variety in Vegetables and Side Dishes   71

A Bounty of Beverages   79

Savory Salads, Dressings and Sauces   87

Breads and Other Baked Treats   99

Cook-at-Table Specials   109

Cooking with a Foreign Flavor   121

Delectable Desserts   133

Index   155

ABOUT THIS BOOK...

Welcome to the wonderful world of portable electric cookery! This cookbook—like all good cookbooks—should be approached as cooking itself ought to be: with forethought. First, be certain that you have read all the instructions concerning the care and use of your new appliance on the first eight pages of this book—learn how to operate the appliance for best service and best results before you cook with it. Second, browse through the book—cookbooks make interesting reading—and find recipes that appeal to you. Finally, when you are ready to try your first recipe, read it all the way through to make sure that you understand it and that you have all the ingredients in the house. Assemble those ingredients before you start to work.

Remember—following the instructions in the recipe is important. So are careful measuring and the use of standard measuring cups and spoons. And bear in mind this cardinal rule of cooking: the time to experiment with a recipe, to change ingredients or to try for a difference in flavor, is the *second* time you make the dish, not the first.

Portable electric appliances make cooking a joy. With an electric cooker and deep fryer or an electric frypan, cooking at the table becomes a practical pleasure. Use them, as well, to keep food piping hot at the dinner table or for buffet service.

With an electric knife, carving is quick and easy. In the kitchen, a Mixmaster Mixer and a blender are like having extra pairs of hands. They simplify the preparation of recipes you never dared try before and help you cook old favorites with new ease and speed.

You're sure to enjoy using your new appliance—and this new cookbook. Have fun!

APPEALING APPETIZERS

Delectable spreads and dips, zesty pâtés, savory molded delicacies, plus a host of cook-on-the-spot hot appetizers—all these and more are here for the trying. Once you've tried them, they'll be favorites of yours for any company-coming occasion. Let your Sunbeam Appliances play their important roles—mixing, cooking, keeping hot appetizers really hot.

PARTY PATE
3⅓ cups pâté

1 can (3 or 4 ounces) chopped mushrooms
1 envelope unflavored gelatin
1 can (10½ ounces) condensed beef bouillon
2 tablespoons brandy
1 teaspoon Worcestershire sauce
2 cans (5 ounces each) liver spread
½ cup pitted ripe olives
½ cup parsley leaves

Drain liquid from mushrooms into Sunbeam Blender. Add gelatin, cover and process at Stir to soften gelatin. Heat ½ cup of the bouillon to boiling. Add to container, cover and continue to process until gelatin is dissolved. If gelatin granules cling to container, use a rubber spatula to push them into the liquid. Add remaining ingredients. Cover and process at Puree until smooth. Pour into a 4-cup mold and chill until firm, 4 hours or overnight. Unmold on chilled serving plate. Garnish as desired. Serve with crackers.

SEASHORE DIP
1 cup

2 packages (3 ounces each) cream cheese
1 can (7 ounces) minced clams
½ teaspoon dried basil
½ teaspoon salt
Dash cayenne pepper
3 sprigs parsley, stems removed
1 teaspoon lemon juice

Crumble cream cheese into Sunbeam Blender. Drain clams, reserving liquid, and add clams to Blender with remaining ingredients. Cover and process at Cream 6 seconds. If a softer mixture is desired, add a little of drained liquid from clams.
Serving style: Serve with potato or corn chips.

Recipe books for new Blenders and Mixers contain information on speed settings for other models in front, Instruction Section.

7

TANTALIZER SPREAD
¾ cup

3 strips bacon
1 small tomato, peeled and
quartered
1 teaspoon prepared mustard
1 package (3 ounces) cream
cheese, cubed
¼ teaspoon celery salt
½ cup blanched almonds

Fry bacon until crisp. Drain on paper towels. Put tomato, mustard, cream cheese and celery salt into Sunbeam Blender; cover and process at Mix until smooth. Add almonds and bacon; cover and process at Chop only until almonds are chopped.

CLUB CHEDDAR DIP
1½ cups

1 tablespoon Worcestershire
sauce
½ teaspoon dry mustard
2 ounces Gruyère cheese, cubed
1 bottle (7 ounces) beer
Dash cayenne pepper
½ pound mild Cheddar cheese,
cubed

Put all ingredients except Cheddar into Sunbeam Blender; cover and process at Chop until smooth. Remove Feeder Cap and add Cheddar cheese cubes gradually; continue to process at Blend until smooth.

SHRIMP SOUP DIP
1½ cups

1 can (10 ounces) frozen
condensed cream of shrimp
soup, defrosted
1 package (3 ounces) cream
cheese, softened and quartered
1 teaspoon lemon juice
¼ teaspoon garlic powder

Put all ingredients into Sunbeam Blender; cover and process at Beat until smooth.

BRAUNSCHWEIGER
SPREAD
1½ cups

2 tablespoons pickle juice
½ pound Braunschweiger, cubed
¼ medium onion
1 rib celery, cut up
⅛ teaspoon Tabasco sauce
2 sprigs parsley

Put all ingredients into Sunbeam Blender; cover and process at Beat until smooth.

CRAB MEAT SPREAD
1 cup

3 tablespoons light cream
1 tablespoon prepared
horseradish
1 cup crab meat, picked over

Put all ingredients into Sunbeam Blender; cover and process at Cream until smooth.

SHERRY CHEDDAR CHEESE
1½ cups

⅓ cup sherry
½ cup heavy cream
¼ teaspoon mace
½ pound Cheddar cheese, cubed
1 tablespoon chives, snipped

Put sherry, cream, mace and half the Cheddar into Sunbeam Blender; cover and process at Chop until smooth. While processing, remove Feeder Cap from lid and add remaining Cheddar and chives. Continue processing at Blend until smooth.

CLAM DIP
1¼ cups

1 can (6 ounces) minced clams
1 tablespoon clam juice
6 drops Tabasco sauce
½ teaspoon Worcestershire
sauce
¼ teaspoon salt
½ teaspoon onion salt
1 cup creamed cottage cheese

Drain clams and put into Sunbeam Blender with remaining ingredients. Cover and process at Beat until smooth. Chill before serving.

LOBSTER SPREAD
1½ cups

¼ cup mayonnaise
1 cup cooked lobster meat, cubed
3 hard-cooked eggs, shelled
¼ teaspoon salt
Dash Tabasco sauce

Put all ingredients into Sunbeam Blender; cover and process at Beat until smooth.

Recipe books for new Blenders and Mixers contain information on speed settings for other models in front, Instruction Section.

EGG AND AVOCADO DIP
3 cups

3 ripe avocados, peeled and
cut into chunks
6 hard-cooked egg yolks
¾ teaspoon chili powder
½ small onion, quartered
3 tablespoons parsley flakes
3 tablespoons cider vinegar
1½ teaspoons salt
⅛ teaspoon black pepper

Put all ingredients into Sunbeam Blender. Cover and process at Puree until smooth.

STUFFED MUSHROOMS
8 servings

8 medium mushrooms
¼ cup salad oil
2 tablespoons minced onion
½ cup bread crumbs
¼ teaspoon Tabasco sauce
¼ teaspoon crushed thyme
¼ cup sherry

Carefully twist off stems from mushroom caps, leaving caps intact. Chop enough stems to make 2 tablespoons. Preheat Multi-Cooker Frypan to 300°. Heat 2 tablespoons of the oil in Frypan. Add onion and mushroom stems and sauté gently until onion is tender. Add bread crumbs, Tabasco, thyme, and mix well. Remove from heat and fill mushroom caps with stuffing. Wipe Frypan with a paper towel. Set

Frypan at 300°. Heat remaining 2 tablespoons oil. Add stuffed mushrooms, cap-side down, and sauté about 3 minutes. Add sherry, cover and simmer gently about 10 minutes or until tender. Serve piping hot.

APPETIZER MEATBALLS
50 portions

1 pound ground beef
¾ teaspoon salt
1 tablespoon minced onion
½ cup soft bread crumbs
¼ cup milk
1 tablespoon flour
2 tablespoons butter
3 tablespoons molasses
3 tablespoons prepared mustard
3 tablespoons vinegar
¼ cup ketchup
¼ teaspoon thyme

In a large mixing bowl combine meat, salt, onion, bread crumbs and milk. Toss lightly until well blended. Shape into bite-sized meatballs. Roll in flour. Preheat Multi-Cooker Frypan to 320°. Melt butter in hot Frypan. Brown meatballs on all sides in hot butter. Remove meatballs as they brown. Combine remaining ingredients and stir into Frypan. Stir well to bring up bits of browned meat from bottom of Frypan. Bring to a boil. Add meatballs to sauce. Cover and simmer very gently 8 to 10 minutes, stirring occasionally. Serve as hot appetizers with toothpicks.

Recipe books for new Blenders and Mixers
contain information on speed settings for
other models in front, Instruction Section.

SWISS CHEESE DIP
2½ cups

½ cup mayonnaise
2 tablespoons chili sauce
1 cup creamed cottage cheese
1 small wedge onion
¼ teaspoon salt
¼ teaspoon celery salt
1 cup cubed Swiss cheese

Put all ingredients except Swiss cheese into Sunbeam Blender; cover and process at Beat until smooth. Remove Feeder Cap and add Swiss cheese cubes gradually. Process at Beat until smooth.

SHRIMP DIP
2 cups

¼ cup milk
1 cup mayonnaise
1 tablespoon Worcestershire sauce
¼ teaspoon garlic salt
3 drops Tabasco sauce
1 small onion, quartered
1 can (5 ounces) shrimp, drained
½ pound Cheddar cheese, cubed

Put all ingredients into Sunbeam Blender; cover and process at Chop until smooth. Chill.

SOUTH-OF-THE-BORDER DIP
1 cup

1 medium avocado, peeled, cubed
2 tomatoes, peeled, seeded, cubed
3 green pepper rings, ½ inch wide
½ medium onion, sliced
2 tablespoons lime juice
½ teaspoon dry mustard
½ teaspoon Worcestershire sauce
Dash Tabasco sauce
½ teaspoon salt

Combine all ingredients in Sunbeam Blender. Cover and process at Cream 1 minute. Serve with corn chips.

ROQUEFORT CHEESE DIP
1¼ cups

1 tablespoon cream
1 teaspoon Worcestershire sauce
1 teaspoon lemon juice
1 cup creamed cottage cheese
1 package (3 ounces) Roquefort cheese, cubed

Put all ingredients into Sunbeam Blender; cover and process at Cream until smooth.

PIMIENTO CHEESE DIP
1½ cups

½ cup mayonnaise
1 jar (2 ounces) pimientos, with
liquid
2 teaspoons Worcestershire
sauce
1 teaspoon prepared mustard
1 cup Cheddar cheese, cubed

Put first four ingredients and half the Cheddar into Sunbeam Blender; cover and process at Chop until smooth. Remove Feeder Cap and add remaining Cheddar. Process at Chop until smooth and creamy.

RED CHEESE BALL
one 3-inch ball

½ teaspoon Worcestershire
sauce
¼ cup pitted ripe olives
1 package (3 ounces) cream
cheese, cubed
½ pound Cheddar cheese, cubed
Dash each of onion, garlic and
celery salts
½ cup dried beef

Put all ingredients except dried beef into Sunbeam Blender. Cover and process at Beat until smooth. Remove from Blender and shape into a ball, wrap in foil and refrigerate until needed. About 30 minutes before serving, remove foil from cheese ball, re-shape if necessary. Blender-chop dried beef. Roll cheese ball in beef until completely coated.

EGGPLANT DIP
5 cups

3 large eggplants
1¼ cups lemon juice
1 cup oil (sesame seed or
peanut oil)
4 cloves garlic, crushed
2 teaspoons salt
2 bunches radishes
3 bunches scallions
Poori (see page 128)

Cut stem and green hull from top of each eggplant. Bake eggplants in preheated 400° F. oven about 1 hour or until flesh is soft and skin crisp. Let cool slightly. Scoop pulp out of skins into large bowl of Mixmaster Mixer. Beat at No. 7 until thoroughly blended. Turn to No. 2 and slowly beat in lemon juice and oil alternately. Add garlic and salt and blend in thoroughly. Taste and adjust seasoning if necessary. Serve as an appetizer at room temperature, surrounded by radishes, scallions and broken chunks of Poori to dip into the mixture.

Good to know: In Lebanon, where this unusual use of eggplant originated, this dip is called Baba Ghannouj.

Recipe books for new Blenders and Mixers
contain information on speed settings for
other models in front, Instruction Section.

13

FRIED CHICKEN WINGS
4 servings

¼ cup soy sauce
¾ cup sherry
½ teaspoon ground ginger
2 cloves garlic, mashed
1 pound chicken wings
Flour
Cooking oil for frying

Combine soy sauce, sherry, ginger and garlic in a bowl. Add chicken wings and let stand about 4 hours, turning wings occasionally. Drain off liquid into a measuring cup. Combine ½ cup of the mixture with ¼ cup flour to make a smooth batter. Coat chicken wings with flour, then dip into batter. Preheat Sunbeam Cooker and Deep Fryer to 375°. Fry wings in hot oil until they are crisp, tender and golden, about 5 to 6 minutes. Lift out basket to drain. Drain on paper towels.

QUICK PATE
24 appetizer servings

2 envelopes unflavored gelatin
2 cans (10½ ounces each)
condensed bouillon
6 tablespoons brandy
4 cans (4¾ ounces each)
liver pâté

Sprinkle gelatin over ½ cup cold water in a saucepan. Place over moderate heat and stir until gelatin dissolves. Add bouillon and brandy. Chill mixture in refrigerator until it is the consistency of unbeaten egg white. Add liver pâté and beat with Mixmaster Hand Mixer or Mixmaster Mixer until mixture is well blended and smooth. Turn mixture into a 5-cup mold or small loaf pan. Chill until firm. Unmold and garnish as desired.

CHEESE PUFFS
16 to 18 puffs

Cooking oil or shortening for
deep frying
2 egg whites
1 cup grated Parmesan cheese
2 tablespoons finely chopped
parsley
1 teaspoon finely grated onion
3 tablespoons flour
¼ teaspoon celery seed
Dash cayenne pepper
Fine dry bread crumbs
Paprika

Heat oil or shortening in Sunbeam Cooker and Deep Fryer to 375°. Place egg whites in small bowl of Mixmaster Mixer. Beat at highest speed until whites are stiff but not dry. Combine Parmesan, parsley, onion, flour, celery seeds and cayenne. Fold into beaten egg whites. With 2 teaspoons, form mixture into small balls. Roll in crumbs, sprinkle with paprika. Lower slowly into preheated fat. Fry until browned, turning. Drain on paper towels. Serve piping hot.

SUPERB SOUPS

Here are soups for all seasons—cold delights to wait in the refrigerator until summer suppertime, long-simmered soups to grace winter-weather meals. Your Sunbeam Blender is a handy helper with the cold soups; use your Sunbeam Cooker and Deep Fryer for the hot ones—in fact, bring it to the table and dish the soups up on the spot. Handy for seconds.

CREAM OF CARROT SOUP
4 servings

2 cups carrot pieces
1 onion, quartered
1½ cups milk
1 cup chicken stock
⅓ cup butter or margarine
2 whole cloves
2 tablespoons flour
½ cup cream

Place carrot, onion, milk and chicken stock in Sunbeam Blender. Cover and process at Chop. Drain through sieve and reserve liquid. Sauté vegetables in butter, add ½ cup water and cloves and cook until tender. Remove cloves; put vegetables, flour, and half of reserved liquid into Blender; cover and process at Puree until smooth. Pour into saucepan, add remaining liquid and cook slowly about 10 minutes, stirring constantly. Add cream and season to taste.

BEEF VEGETABLE SOUP
8 to 10 servings

2 pounds shin of beef, with
bone and meat
2 tablespoons salt
1½ cups diced celery
1½ cups diced carrots
1½ cups diced raw potatoes
1½ cups diced onions
2 cups frozen or canned
mixed vegetables
2½ cups canned tomatoes
⅛ teaspoon pepper
2 tablespoons snipped parsley

Cut meat into small cubes. Put soup bone, meat, 3 quarts water and salt into Sunbeam Cooker and Deep Fryer. Set Dial at 300° until soup is boiling. Skim off top of liquid and discard. Turn Dial to Simmer. Cover and simmer 3 hours. Add remaining ingredients, except parsley. Cook 45 minutes or until vegetables are tender. Season to taste. Serve in soup bowls with a garnish of parsley.

Recipe books for new Blenders and Mixers
contain information on speed settings for
other models in front, Instruction Section.

CURRIED PEA SOUP
8 servings

2 tablespoons soft butter
1 tablespoon flour
2½ cups chicken broth
1 chicken bouillon cube
½ cup milk
1½ cups cooked peas
1½ teaspoons curry powder
Salt to taste

Put butter, flour and chicken broth into Sunbeam Blender; cover and process at Beat until smooth. Empty into saucepan. Put remaining ingredients into Blender; cover and process at Puree until smooth. Add to saucepan; mix well. Simmer until thick, stirring constantly.

CREAM OF MUSHROOM SOUP
4 servings

⅛ medium onion
1 cup sliced mushrooms
2 tablespoons butter or margarine
2 cups milk
2 tablespoons flour
⅓ cup celery pieces
½ teaspoon salt
Dash pepper

Place onion in Sunbeam Blender; cover and process at Chop. Sauté mushrooms and onion in butter. Put remaining ingredients into Blender; cover and process at Mix until smooth. Add mushrooms and onions. Process at Chop until mushrooms are finely chopped. Pour into saucepan and cook until thickened.

BORSCHT
4 servings

2 cups sour cream, divided
½ small lemon, peeled and seeded
¼ teaspoon salt
¼ teaspoon celery salt
¼ teaspoon onion salt
1 cup diced cooked beets

Put 1¾ cups sour cream and all remaining ingredients into Sunbeam Blender; cover and process at Puree until smooth. Serve icy cold, garnished with remaining sour cream.

TUNA BISQUE
6 servings

2½ cups milk, divided
1 can (10½ ounces) condensed cream of asparagus soup
1 can (10½ ounces) condensed cream of mushroom soup
5 tablespoons sherry
1 can (7 ounces) tuna, drained and flaked

Put 1 cup milk into Sunbeam Blender; add soups and sherry. Cover and process at Puree until smooth. Pour into a saucepan and add remaining milk and tuna. Simmer about 10 minutes or until thoroughly heated.

GAZPACHO
6 servings

1/2 pound onions, peeled and
quartered
6 tomatoes, peeled and quartered
1/2 cup red wine
2 1/2 tablespoons olive oil
1 tablespoon paprika
1 clove garlic
1 cucumber, peeled, quartered
and thinly sliced
2 black olives, pitted and sliced
Salt, pepper
Parsley, finely chopped
Croutons

Combine onions, tomatoes, red wine, olive oil, paprika and garlic clove. Place half into Sunbeam Blender; cover and process at Puree until smooth. Empty into saucepan and repeat process with remaining half of mixture. Simmer 10 minutes. Stir the cucumber and olives into the soup, season to taste; chill. Sprinkle the soup liberally with finely chopped parsley and garnish with croutons.

SUPERB ASPARAGUS SOUP
4 servings

1 package (10 ounces) frozen
asparagus
1 cup chicken broth
2 raw mushrooms, quartered
1 tablespoon minced onion
1/2 teaspoon salt
1/4 teaspoon chili powder
1/2 teaspoon lemon juice
1 cup cream, light or heavy

Break up frozen asparagus and place in Sunbeam Blender. Add broth, mushrooms, onion, seasonings and lemon juice. Cover and process at Puree 1 minute. Add cream, process at Stir 30 seconds. Serve cold, or heat in double boiler.

SUPREME TOMATO SOUP
6 to 8 servings

2 hard-cooked egg yolks
1 medium onion, quartered
2 tablespoons butter or
margarine
1 package (3 ounces) cream
cheese, cubed
2 cans (10 1/2 ounces each)
condensed tomato soup
3 cups milk
1/8 teaspoon garlic powder
1/2 teaspoon paprika

Blender-grate egg yolks and re-

*Recipe books for new Blenders and Mixers
contain information on speed settings for
other models in front, Instruction Section.*

17

serve. Chop onion in Sunbeam Blender, sauté in butter. Combine sautéed onion with remaining ingredients and put half of this mixture into Sunbeam Blender; cover and process at Cream until smooth. Empty into a saucepan. Repeat process with remaining half of ingredients. Heat, stirring constantly, but do not boil. Garnish with egg yolks.

CREAM OF CELERY SOUP
6 servings

l medium onion, quartered
⅓ cup butter or margarine
6 to 8 ribs celery cut into
1-inch pieces
2 potatoes, peeled, cubed
½ bay leaf
½ teaspoon salt
¼ teaspoon pepper
2 cups milk, divided
8 sprigs parsley
½ cup heavy cream

Blender-chop onion. Sauté in butter until golden brown. Put celery, potatoes, 1 cup water, bay leaf, salt and pepper into saucepan; cover and cook slowly 30 minutes or until soft. Remove bay leaf. Put 1 cup milk into Sunbeam Blender with half of cooked vegetable mixture and onions; cover and process at

Puree until smooth. Pour into saucepan. Repeat with remaining mixture. When mixture is smooth, add parsley and process only until chopped. Add to mixture in saucepan and heat slowly. Add cream and seasoning before serving.

VICHYSSOISE
4 to 6 servings

2 cups peeled, cubed potatoes
¾ cup leek pieces
2 cups chicken broth
1 cup milk
1 teaspoon salt
Dash white pepper
1 cup light cream
Chopped chives

Blender-chop potatoes and leek. Pour into a saucepan and cook until potatoes are tender. Put remaining ingredients, except cream, into Sunbeam Blender. Add cooked mixture; cover and process at Puree until smooth. Pour into bowl and stir in cream. Chill thoroughly before serving. Garnish with chopped chives.

FROSTY SOUR-CREAM TOMATO SOUP
4 servings

2 cans (10½ ounces each)
condensed tomato soup
1 cup sour cream
Snipped parsley

Recipe books for new Blenders and Mixers
contain information on speed settings for
other models in front, Instruction Section.

Put soup, sour cream and 1½ cups water in Sunbeam Blender. Process at Puree until smooth. Chill several hours before serving. Garnish with parsley.

TUNA CHOWDER
6 to 8 servings

1 medium onion, cut in eighths
2 tablespoons butter or
margarine
2 cans (7 ounces each) tuna,
drained and flaked
12 sprigs parsley
1 cup milk
2 cans (10 ounces each) frozen
cream of potato soup, thawed
¼ teaspoon pepper

Blender-chop onion with 1 cup water. Drain, reserving liquid. Melt butter in saucepan and sauté onion until soft. Add flaked tuna and remove from heat. Put parsley, milk, reserved water, soup and seasonings into Blender. Cover and process at Chop until parsley is chopped. Pour into saucepan; mix well with onions and tuna. Simmer over low heat about 15 minutes. If a thinner chowder is desired, an additional cup of water or milk may be added.

SPRINGTIME PEA SOUP
4 servings

1 package frozen peas
1 cup chicken broth
1 large lettuce leaf, cut up
1 tablespoon minced onion
½ teaspoon salt
¼ teaspoon white pepper
⅛ teaspoon cardamom
1 cup cream, light or heavy

Break up frozen peas and place in Sunbeam Blender. Add broth, lettuce, onion, seasonings; process at Puree 1 minute. Add cream, process at Stir 20 seconds. Serve cold, or heat in double boiler.

MEXICAN MEATBALL SOUP
6 servings

1 pound ground beef
¾ teaspoon salt
¾ teaspoon chili powder
1 small onion, very finely minced
1 cup dry bread crumbs
⅓ cup pine nuts
1 egg, beaten
⅓ cup sherry, divided
2 cans (10½ ounces each) beef
bouillon or consommé
1 bay leaf

Mix first 7 ingredients and 1 tablespoon sherry. Shape mixture into tiny meatballs about 1 inch in diameter. Put bouillon, 2 soup cans water and bay leaf into Sunbeam Cooker and Deep Fryer. Set Dial at 300°. When mixture is boiling, drop in meatballs, a few at a time, so that boiling remains constant. Reduce heat, cover and simmer until meatballs are tender, about 25 minutes. Just before serving, remove bay leaf and stir in remaining sherry.

CHICKEN GUMBO SOUP
4 to 6 servings

2 tablespoons bacon fat
1 medium-sized onion, diced
½ cup diced green pepper
2 stalks celery, sliced
1 quart chicken or turkey stock
2 cups canned tomatoes
1 teaspoon salt
⅛ teaspoon pepper
⅓ cup uncooked rice
1 cup canned or cooked okra
1 to 2 cups diced cooked chicken or turkey
2 tablespoons chopped parsley

Set Dial of Sunbeam Cooker and Deep Fryer at 300°. Melt fat. Add onion, green pepper and celery. Fry, stirring constantly until partially tender, but *do not brown*. Add chicken stock, tomatoes, salt, pepper, rice and okra. When mixture is boiling, turn Dial to Simmer. Cover and simmer about 40 minutes. Add cooked chicken and heat. Serve with chopped parsley.

ONION SOUP
6 to 8 servings

1½ pounds yellow onions
¼ cup butter or margarine
2 tablespoons salad oil
1 teaspoon salt
Pinch sugar
2 tablespoons flour
2 quarts canned beef bouillon
½ cup dry white wine
Toasted French bread slices
Grated Swiss or Parmesan cheese

Peel and cut onions into very thin slices. Set Dial of Sunbeam Cooker and Deep Fryer at 300°. Melt butter with salad oil. Add onions and simmer about 10 minutes. Sprinkle salt and sugar over onions. Raise heat to 325° and cook until onions are tender and golden brown, stirring occasionally. Sprinkle flour over top of onions and stir 2 minutes. Stir in beef bouillon and wine. Taste and add salt and pepper if necessary. Cover and simmer 30 to 40 minutes. Serve piping hot with slices of toasted French bread and Swiss or Parmesan.

SPLIT PEA SOUP
8 servings

2 cups dried split peas
1 onion, sliced
2 stalks celery, sliced
1 carrot, sliced
1 ham bone

Recipe books for new Blenders and Mixers contain information on speed settings for other models in front, Instruction Section.

21

¼ bay leaf
3 cups milk
2 tablespoons butter or
    margarine
1 teaspoon salt
⅛ teaspoon pepper
Chopped parsley

Wash peas. Soak in cold water several hours or overnight. (If quick-cooking peas are used, do not soak.) Put peas, 2 quarts water, onion, celery, carrot, ham bone and bay leaf in Sunbeam Cooker and Deep Fryer. Bring to boil at 300°. Set Dial at Simmer. Cover and simmer about 2 hours or until peas are tender. Turn off heat and let cool slightly. Remove ham bone. Place part of mixture into Sunbeam Blender. Cover and process at Puree until smooth. Continue to process remaining mixture. Return smooth mixture to Sunbeam Cooker and Deep Fryer. Add milk, butter, salt and pepper. Heat at 300°, but do not boil. Sprinkle with chopped parsley before serving.

SUMMER TOMATO SOUP
8 servings

¼ pound butter or
    margarine
2 tablespoons olive oil
1 large onion, thinly sliced
½ teaspoon dried thyme
½ teaspoon dried basil
Salt, pepper
2½ pounds fresh, ripe tomatoes,
    quartered
or 1 can (2 pounds 3 ounces)
    tomatoes, preferably Italian
    style
3 tablespoons tomato paste
¼ cup flour
3¾ cups fresh or canned
    chicken broth
1 teaspoon sugar
1 cup heavy cream

Preheat Sunbeam Cooker and Deep Fryer to second M in Simmer. Add butter; when melted add olive oil. Add onion, thyme, basil, salt and pepper. Cook, stirring occasionally until onion is wilted. Add tomatoes and tomato paste; stir to blend. Cook 10 minutes. Place flour in small bowl; add about 5 tablespoons of the broth, stirring to blend. Stir into tomato mixture. Add remainder of broth; cook 20 minutes, stirring frequently. Process soup in quarters or thirds at Puree in Sunbeam Blender. Return to Cooker and stir in sugar and cream. Heat until serving temperature.

MAGIC WITH MEATS

Hearty and flavorsome family fare, masterpieces for entertaining, thrifty dishes for the times you're particularly budget-conscious—here are many ways with meat, the center of the meal. Let your Multi-Cooker Frypan, your Cooker and Deep Fryer, your Sunbeam Knife all serve as your willing helpers in getting the meal on the table swiftly, easily—and with flair!

PORK CHOPS
IN VERMOUTH
6 servings

¼ cup flour
1 teaspoon salt
½ teaspoon thyme
¼ teaspoon pepper
6 pork chops, cut ½ inch thick
2 tablespoons butter or
margarine
2 tablespoons salad oil
½ cup dry vermouth or dry
white wine

Combine flour, salt, thyme and pepper. Cut as much fat from pork chops as possible. Dust pork chops with flour mixture. Preheat Multi-Cooker Frypan to 340°. Heat butter and oil in hot Frypan. Add pork chops and cook until golden brown on both sides. Drain off all fat from skillet. Add vermouth. Reduce heat to Simmer. Cover and cook 30 minutes or until pork chops are tender. Add more wine during cooking time if necessary.

GOURMET PORK CHOPS
4 servings

4 slices Swiss cheese, diced
¼ cup chopped parsley
½ cup chopped fresh
mushrooms
4 loin pork chops, 1 inch thick
1 egg, slightly beaten
½ cup packaged dry bread
crumbs
3 tablespoons shortening
½ cup Chablis

Combine cheese, parsley and mushrooms. Slit each pork chop from the bone almost to the fat, making a pocket. Fill pockets with cheese mixture. Preheat Multi-Cooker Frypan to 340°. Dip pork chops into egg, then bread crumbs. Melt shortening in Frypan and brown chops well on both sides. Add Chablis. Reduce heat to Simmer. Cover and cook 45 minutes or until chops are tender. Remove to hot platter. Season sauce with salt to taste, pour over chops.

Recipe books for new Blenders and Mixers
contain information on speed settings for
other models in front, Instruction Section.

23

SWEET AND SOUR PORK
4 servings

3 large green peppers
1 egg, beaten
2 tablespoons flour
½ teaspoon salt
Dash pepper
1 pound lean pork, cut into
½-inch cubes
½ cup salad oil
1 clove garlic, crushed
1 cup chicken bouillon, divided
1 can (8¾ ounces) pineapple
tidbits, drained
2½ tablespoons cornstarch
2 teaspoons soy sauce
½ cup vinegar
½ cup sugar
Hot cooked rice

Remove seeds from green peppers and cut into large chunks with Sunbeam Knife. Cook in boiling water 3 minutes, drain and set aside. Beat together egg, flour, salt and pepper in a small bowl to make a batter. Add pork chunks to batter and mix lightly until every piece of pork is coated. Preheat Multi-Cooker Frypan to 360°. Add oil and garlic. Separate pieces of pork with a fork and drop one piece at a time into the hot oil. Brown pork chunks on all sides. Remove pork and pour out all except 1 tablespoon of the oil. Return pork chunks to Frypan. Add ⅓ cup of the chicken bouillon. Reduce heat to Simmer, cover and cook 10 minutes. Add green pepper and pineapple. Combine cornstarch, soy sauce, vinegar, sugar and remaining chicken bouillon. Add to pork in Frypan and cook, stirring constantly until mixture thickens and is very hot and bubbling. Serve immediately with hot cooked rice.

PORK AND CABBAGE SKILLET
4 servings

1 medium head new cabbage
1½ pounds cubed lean pork
2 tablespoons butter or
margarine
2 tablespoons olive oil
¾ cup finely chopped onion
1 medium clove garlic, mashed
⅓ cup finely chopped green
pepper
2 cups peeled, seeded, chopped
tomatoes
½ teaspoon thyme
Salt, pepper

Shred cabbage coarsely with Sunbeam Knife and reserve. Preheat Multi-Cooker Frypan to 350°. In the Frypan, lightly brown pork cubes in the combined butter and oil. Remove pork cubes with slotted spoon; keep warm. In Frypan, cook onion, garlic and pepper until soft but not browned, stirring frequently. Add tomatoes, thyme, salt and pepper to taste. Reduce heat to 275°. Return pork cubes to Frypan. Cover Frypan and simmer 30 minutes, stirring occasionally. Add cabbage and cook uncovered, stirring constantly but gently, 5 to 10 minutes longer or until cabbage is slightly cooked but still crisp.

BARBECUED
PORK CHOPS
6 servings

1 medium onion, quartered
1 clove garlic, halved
1 stalk celery with leaves,
cut into chunks
1 small green pepper, seeded,
cut into chunks
1 cup ketchup
2 tablespoons wine vinegar
1 tablespoon Worcestershire
sauce
1 teaspoon salt
¼ teaspoon pepper
6 lean pork chops, 1 inch thick

Place all ingredients except chops in Sunbeam Blender. Cover and process at Chop until vegetables are very finely chopped. Set aside. Preheat Multi-Cooker Frypan to 360°. Rub a small amount of the fat from the chops over bottom of Frypan. Add chops and brown well on both sides. Pour mixture from Blender over top of pork chops. Cover, reduce heat to Simmer and cook 45 minutes

or until chops are tender. Turn occasionally during cooking.

PORK TENDERLOIN
IN CREAM
4 servings

2 tablespoons shortening
1 clove garlic
2 whole pork tenderloins
Flour
½ teaspoon salt
½ cup plus 2 tablespoons
sour cream

Heat fat to 320° in Multi-Cooker Frypan. Sauté garlic until golden; remove. With Sunbeam Knife cut tenderloins into 2-inch pieces. Dip each piece in flour; brown on all sides in Frypan. Turn Dial to Simmer. Add salt and ½ cup sour cream; simmer, covered, 40 minutes or until tender. Just before serving, stir additional 2 tablespoons sour cream into gravy.

PAPRIKA HAM
4 to 6 servings

2 tablespoons fat
1 small onion, sliced
2 cups cubed cooked ham
1 can (8 ounces) tomato sauce
2 tablespoons prepared mustard
1 teaspoon paprika
1 cup sour cream
Hot cooked noodles

Recipe books for new Blenders and Mixers contain information on speed settings for other models in front, Instruction Section.

25

Preheat Multi-Cooker Frypan to 340°. Heat fat in Frypan. Add onion and cook until just tender. Stir in ham. Combine tomato sauce, mustard and paprika. Pour over ham. Cover. Reduce heat to Simmer and cook 30 minutes. Stir in sour cream, and heat but *do not boil*. Serve over hot cooked noodles.

SAUERKRAUT SKILLET
4 to 5 servings

1 pound bulk pork sausage
½ teaspoon ground juniper
berries (optional)
1½ cups sauerkraut, drained
and rinsed
1¼ cups sour cream
Salt, pepper, paprika
¾ cup garlic croutons

Preheat Multi-Cooker Frypan to 350°. Sauté sausage in Frypan until it begins to cook but is still light in color. Lower heat to 300° and cook, stirring frequently until the sausage begins to brown. Sprinkle with juniper berries and stir. Lower heat to 250°. Add sauerkraut and sour cream and cook 15 minutes. Sprinkle lightly with salt and pepper; taste and season if necessary. Sprinkle with paprika, then with croutons, and serve from Frypan.

Try it this way: If desired, use only ½ pound sausage, and add ½ pound ground ham.

PORK AND SAUERKRAUT
6 servings

2 pounds boneless pork shoulder
2 cups chopped onions
1 clove garlic, minced
1 teaspoon dried dillweed
1 teaspoon caraway seed
1 tablespoon salt
1 beef bouillon cube
1 tablespoon paprika
1 can (1 pound 11 ounces)
sauerkraut, drained
2 cups sour cream
Hot cooked potatoes

Cut meat into 1½-inch cubes, discard fat. In Sunbeam Cooker and Deep Fryer combine pork, onion, garlic, dill, caraway seed, salt, bouillon cube and ½ cup boiling water. Bring to a boil. Lower heat to Simmer, cover and cook 1 hour. Stir in paprika until dissolved. Add sauerkraut and mix well. Simmer, covered, 1 hour longer or until meat is tender. Turn heat off. Gradually stir in sour cream. Turn up heat to I of Simmer and heat mixture through, but *do not boil*. Serve with hot cooked potatoes.

OSSO BUCO
MILANESE STYLE
4 servings

3 tablespoons salad oil
4 veal shanks, 4 inches long,
with meat

3 tablespoons flour
1 clove garlic, chopped
½ cup chicken broth
¼ teaspoon Tabasco sauce
6 strips lemon peel
3 anchovy fillets, chopped
Chopped parsley
Cooked bow-shaped pasta

Preheat Multi-Cooker Frypan to 360°. Heat oil in Frypan. Roll veal shanks in flour. Place shanks in Frypan and cook until lightly browned, turning occasionally. Add garlic, broth, 1 cup water and Tabasco. Cover. Reduce heat to Simmer and cook about 1 hour or until veal is tender. Add more water if necessary during cooking time. Add lemon strips and anchovy fillets and simmer 5 minutes. Serve, topped with a generous sprinkling of parsley, with cooked pasta.

LEMON VEAL STEW
6 servings

2 pounds stewing veal, cubed
½ cup sliced onion
1 bay leaf
3 peppercorns
2 teaspoons salt
4 tablespoons butter
1 cup sliced mushrooms
¼ cup flour
3 tablespoons lemon juice
2 tablespoons chopped parsley

Place 4 cups of water in Sunbeam Cooker and Deep Fryer and heat to 300°. Add first 5 ingredients; bring to a boil. Turn

Dial to first M of Simmer; cook, covered, skimming off foam as it appears, until meat is tender. Remove bay leaf and peppercorns. In Multi-Cooker Frypan heated to 320°, melt butter; sauté mushrooms in butter until very lightly browned. Add flour and lemon juice; mix well and add to veal stew. Continue to cook until thickened. Sprinkle with chopped parsley.

SPANISH LAMB STEW
6 servings

1 tablespoon olive oil
2 pounds breast of lamb
⅓ cup flour
1 teaspoon cider vinegar
1 bay leaf
3½ teaspoons salt
¾ cup chopped onion
½ cup chopped green pepper
½ cup rice
1 package (10 ounces) frozen peas, thawed
1 can (1 pound, 3 ounces) tomatoes
½ teaspoon thyme
2 eggs
1 tablespoon olive oil

Preheat Sunbeam Cooker and Deep Fryer to 350°. Add olive oil. Cut lamb into 1½-inch pieces. Dredge lamb in flour and brown. Turn Cooker and Deep Fryer to R in Simmer. Remove lamb. Drain fat and oil from Cooker and replace lamb. Add vinegar, 3 cups hot water, bay leaf and salt. Cover and cook about 1½ hours or until lamb is almost tender. Add onion, green pepper and rice. Cover, cook 20 minutes. Add peas, tomatoes and thyme. Cover, cook 10 minutes. Combine eggs and oil, beat with a fork. Add to stew and cook, stirring until slightly thickened.

PARTY VEAL ROLLS
4 servings

8 very thin veal cutlets
Salt
Freshly ground black pepper
*1 can (4½ ounces) smoked liver
pâté, chilled*
¼ cup butter or margarine
2 tablespoons brandy
1 clove garlic, chopped
1 onion, chopped
½ cup dry white wine
2 tablespoons snipped parsley

Place veal cutlets between 2 pieces of aluminum foil. Pound until very thin with the flat side of a cleaver. Sprinkle with salt and pepper. Remove pâté carefully from can; cut into 8 equal strips. Place strips of pâté on slices of veal. Roll veal around pâté. Tie rolls with string. Preheat Multi-Cooker Frypan to 340°. Melt butter in hot Frypan. Add veal and cook gently until golden brown on all sides. Warm brandy. Pour over veal and ignite with a wooden match. Allow flames to burn out. Add garlic, onion and wine. Cover, reduce heat to Simmer and cook 30

minutes or until veal rolls are tender. Remove veal to a warmed serving platter. Remove strings. Stir juices in bottom of Frypan and pour over veal. Sprinkle with parsley.

VEAL ITALIENNE
4 servings

8 very thin veal cutlets
*4 thin slices Gruyère or Swiss
cheese*
4 thin slices prosciutto
Salt
Freshly ground black pepper
Flour
*2 tablespoons butter or
margarine*
3 tablespoons olive oil
½ cup dry white wine
½ cup chicken bouillon

Place veal slices between 2 pieces of aluminum foil. Pound until very thin with the flat side of a cleaver. Place a slice of cheese and a slice of prosciutto on 4 pieces of veal. Top with remaining 4 slices of veal. Press edges of veal together to seal, or fasten securely with toothpicks. Season with salt and pepper. Dip in flour and shake off excess. Preheat Multi-Cooker Frypan to 380°. Melt butter and oil in hot Frypan. Add veal and cook 2 or more at a time, turning gently until well browned on both sides. Remove veal to a heated serving platter. Discard most of fat from Frypan, leaving a thin film on the bottom. Pour in wine and bouillon and bring to a boil, stirring up any browned bits of veal on bottom. Return veal to Frypan. Reduce heat to Simmer. Cover and cook about 20 minutes or until veal is tender. Turn veal over once during cooking period. Remove veal to a heated serving platter and pour sauce over the top.

VEAL CHOPS WITH MUSHROOMS
4 servings

⅓ cup butter or margarine
4 veal chops, about 1¼ inches
    thick
½ pound mushrooms, sliced
2 tablespoons lemon juice
½ cup sliced onion
1 small clove garlic, crushed
¼ cup flour
1 teaspoon salt
⅛ teaspoon freshly ground
    pepper
1 can (10½ ounces) condensed
    beef bouillon
⅔ cup dry white wine
1 teaspoon snipped fresh
    tarragon leaves
1 teaspoon snipped chives

Preheat Multi-Cooker Frypan to 340°. Melt butter in Frypan. Brown chops lightly on both sides. Remove chops and set aside. Sprinkle mushroom slices with lemon juice. Place in Frypan with onion and garlic. Cook, stirring until golden, about 5

minutes. Remove mushrooms and onions, and reserve. Stir flour, salt and pepper into drippings in Frypan. Gradually stir in bouillon and wine. Add tarragon and chives. Bring to a boil, stirring constantly. Reduce heat to Simmer. Add chops and mushrooms. Cover and simmer 30 minutes or until chops are tender.

BRAISED SHOULDER OF VEAL
4 to 6 servings

4 pounds veal shoulder
2 cloves garlic, thinly sliced
¼ cup butter or margarine
1 teaspoon salt
1 teaspoon freshly ground
    pepper
1 cup bouillon
1 cup dry white wine
1 teaspoon tarragon
1 whole medium onion
½ bay leaf

Have butcher bone, roll and tie veal shoulder. Be sure to take the bones with the meat. Make small incisions in the veal with a sharp knife and insert thin slivers of garlic. Preheat Sunbeam Cooker and Deep Fryer to 300°. Melt butter in hot Cooker. Add veal and brown well on all sides, turning often. Sprinkle with salt and pepper. Add bouillon, white wine, tarragon, onion and bay leaf. Add the veal bones.

29

Cover and reduce heat to Simmer. Simmer gently about 2 hours or until veal is tender. Remove veal to a hot serving platter. Remove strings and slice. Skim fat from juices in Cooker. Discard onion, bay leaf and bones. Serve sauce with veal.

LEG OF LAMB WITH WHITE BEANS
10 servings

1 pound dried navy pea beans
¼ cup butter or margarine
2 cloves garlic
2 pounds onion, thinly sliced
Seasoned salt
½ teaspoon salt
¼ teaspoon freshly ground
  pepper
1 teaspoon rosemary, divided
2 cans (1 pound each) Italian
  plum tomatoes
1 leg of lamb, about 6½ to 7
  pounds

Place beans in Sunbeam Cooker and Deep Fryer. Cover with water. Turn Dial to 400°; bring to a boil. Turn Dial to Simmer and cook 2 minutes. Turn Dial to Off. Cover and let stand about 1 hour. Turn Dial to 300° and bring to a boil. Reduce heat to first M of Simmer and cook, covered, about 1 hour or until beans are just tender. Check liquid during cooking period, adding water if necessary. Drain beans. Place beans in the bottom of a shallow roasting pan. Pre-

heat oven to 325°F. Preheat Multi-Cooker Frypan to 300°. Melt butter in hot Frypan. Crush 1 clove garlic and add to hot butter. Add onions and cook until golden brown, stirring occasionally. Add 2 teaspoons seasoned salt, salt, pepper, ½ teaspoon rosemary and tomatoes. Blend thoroughly with the onion, then blend with beans in bottom of roasting pan. Split remaining clove of garlic and rub over entire surface of lamb. Sprinkle lamb with seasoned salt and remaining rosemary. Place lamb on top of beans. Insert a meat thermometer into heavy part of leg, being careful that it does not touch the bone. Roast, uncovered, about 3 hours or until meat thermometer registers 150°F. Lamb should be slightly pink in the middle. Remove lamb to a carving board. Turn beans into a serving dish. Carve the lamb.

IRISH STEW
4 servings

2 pounds lamb shoulder, cubed
2 onions, quartered
4 small whole carrots, scraped
8 small whole potatoes, peeled
½ head cabbage, coarsely
  shredded
3 tablespoons flour
Salt, pepper
1 cup hot cooked green peas

Place lamb, onions and carrots in Sunbeam Cooker and Deep

Fryer. Add water to cover. Turn Dial to 300° and bring to a boil. Turn to first M in Simmer; cook, covered, skimming off foam as it appears, until meat is tender. Add potatoes; when they are almost done, add cabbage. Mix flour with a little cold water and add, stirring until thickened. Season to taste. Serve on a hot platter with peas on top.

SHERRIED LAMB CHOPS
4 servings

4 shoulder lamb chops, ¾ to 1 inch thick
Salt, pepper
¼ cup salad oil
1 clove garlic
½ cup sherry
1 beef bouillon cube
8 small white onions, peeled
6 carrots, peeled and cut into chunks
4 small potatoes, peeled and halved

Sprinkle chops on both sides with salt and pepper. Preheat Multi-Cooker Frypan to 360°. Add oil and garlic, and heat. Add chops and brown on both sides; remove garlic. Add sherry, ½ cup hot water and bouillon cube. Cover, lower heat to Simmer and cook 30 minutes. Add onions, carrots and potatoes. Sprinkle lightly with salt and pepper. Cover and simmer 20 to 30 minutes or until chops and vegetables are tender.

CRANBERRY SHOULDER LAMB CHOPS
4 servings

4 shoulder lamb chops, about ¾ inch thick
¼ cup flour
½ teaspoon salt
Black pepper, freshly ground
1 tablespoon salad oil
1 clove garlic, halved
¾ cup pineapple juice
1 cup canned cranberries
2 tablespoons sugar
1 teaspoon salt
¾ teaspoon pepper
1 teaspoon Worcestershire sauce

Coat lamb with combined flour, salt and pepper. Preheat Multi-Cooker Frypan to 360°. Add oil; when hot, add chops and brown lightly on both sides. Place remaining ingredients plus ½ cup water in Sunbeam Blender. Cover and process at Beat until smooth. Pour over lamb chops in Frypan. Cover and simmer 45 minutes or until lamb is tender.

SAVORY LAMB CHOPS
4 servings

4 shoulder lamb chops, 1 inch thick
Salt, pepper
2 tablespoons olive oil
¼ cup chopped onion

Recipe books for new Blenders and Mixers contain information on speed settings for other models in front, Instruction Section.

31

½ cup sliced carrots
1 cup peeled, quartered tomatoes
⅓ cup dry sherry
1 cup sliced mushrooms
2 tablespoons butter

Sprinkle chops with salt and pepper. Heat Multi-Cooker Frypan to 340°. Brown the chops in the oil with the onions. Add carrots, tomatoes and sherry. Turn Dial to Simmer. Cover and cook 1 hour or until tender. In a small skillet, sauté mushrooms in butter. Add to chops, cook 5 minutes longer.

MANDARIN LAMB SHANKS
6 servings

1 tablespoon salad oil
6 lamb shanks
Salt, pepper
1 can (10½ ounces) condensed
beef broth
1 cup uncooked rice
1 can (11 ounces) mandarin
orange sections

Heat Multi-Cooker Frypan to 360°. Heat oil. Add lamb shanks and brown well on all sides. Season with salt and pepper. Add 1 cup water. Cover and simmer 1½ hours. Remove lamb shanks. Pour liquid in pan into a measuring cup. Skim off fat from top. Add enough water to make 1 cup liquid. Pour into Frypan. Add beef broth, salt and rice. Return lamb shanks to Frypan. Cover and simmer 25 minutes or

until rice is almost tender. Stir in undrained orange sections and simmer 5 to 10 minutes or until rice is tender. Serve chops and rice piping hot.

LAMB SHOULDER CHOPS, PIZZA STYLE
6 servings

1 tablespoon butter or margarine
6 shoulder lamb chops, cut ¾
inch thick
Salt
Black pepper, freshly ground
Garlic salt
1 can (6 ounces) tomato paste
Oregano
6 slices Mozzarella cheese
Chopped parsley
Fillets of anchovies (optional)

Preheat Multi-Cooker Frypan to 360°. Melt butter in Frypan. Add chops and brown lightly on both sides. Sprinkle each chop with salt, freshly ground pepper and garlic salt. Spread most of the tomato paste over each chop and then sprinkle very lightly with oregano. Top each chop with a slice of Mozzarella. Spread top of cheese with remainder of tomato paste. Sprinkle liberally with chopped parsley and add anchovies. Cover Frypan tightly. Simmer very slowly until chops are tender, about 45 minutes. If chops get dry, add a little tomato juice or water to bottom of Frypan. Serve chops piping hot.

TERIYAKI POT ROAST
4 to 6 servings

3- to 4-pound beef pot roast
1 tablespoon cooking oil
½ teaspoon ground ginger
1 clove garlic, crushed
¼ cup soy sauce
2 medium onions, sliced
1 tablespoon cornstarch

Heat Cooker and Deep Fryer to 350°. Brown the pot roast on all sides in the oil. Reduce heat to first M of Simmer. Mix ginger, garlic and soy sauce with ¼ cup hot water. Add to Cooker and Deep Fryer along with the onions. Cover and simmer about 2½ hours or until meat is tender. Remove meat to hot platter. Mix cornstarch with 2 tablespoons cold water. Add to liquid in Cooker and Deep Fryer and cook, stirring, until thickened. Serve with pot roast.

BARBECUED SHORT RIBS
4 servings

2 tablespoons cooking oil
4 large beef short ribs
1 clove garlic, minced
½ cup diced onions
½ cup diced celery
2 tablespoons cornstarch
1 can (8 ounces) tomato sauce
1 teaspoon salt
⅛ teaspoon pepper
½ teaspoon allspice

1 tablespoon prepared mustard
1 tablespoon vinegar
2 teaspoons sugar

Preheat cooking oil in Sunbeam Cooker and Deep Fryer to 350°. Brown ribs well, 15 to 20 minutes. Add garlic, onions and celery. Stir cornstarch into tomato sauce and add. Stir in ½ cup water and remaining ingredients. Turn Cooker Dial to first M of Simmer. Cook, covered, turning occasionally, 1½ to 2 hours or until ribs are tender.

STEAK DIANE
4 servings

4 sirloin strip steaks, cut ½ inch
thick
Salt
Freshly ground black pepper
1 teaspoon dry mustard
¼ cup butter or margarine
3 tablespoons lemon juice
2 teaspoons snipped chives
1 teaspoon Worcestershire sauce

With a meat mallet or the edge of a heavy saucer pound steaks to ⅓-inch thickness. Sprinkle one side of each steak with salt, pepper and ⅛ teaspoon dry mustard. Pound mixture into meat. Repeat with other side of each steak. Assemble steaks and remaining ingredients on a serving tray. At the table, preheat Multi-Cooker Frypan to 420°. Heat butter in Frypan. Add steaks and cook about 2 minutes on each side. Remove steaks to heated

33

dinner plates. Add lemon juice, chives and Worcestershire to drippings in skillet. Bring to a boil. Serve over top of steaks.

QUICK WINE STEAKS
6 servings

1 package (1 ounce) beef gravy mix
1 cup beef bouillon
1 cup dry red wine
1 tablespoon red currant jelly
6 thin, tender steaks, ¾ inch thick
1 teaspoon salt
¼ teaspoon pepper
¼ cup butter or margarine

Prepare beef gravy mix according to directions on the package, using 1 cup beef bouillon. Stir in wine and jelly. Heat and stir until jelly dissolves. Sprinkle steaks with salt and pepper. Preheat Multi-Cooker Frypan to 420°. Heat butter in hot Frypan. Brown steaks very quickly in hot butter. Pour wine sauce over steaks, lower heat to 380° and cook 3 to 4 minutes or until steaks are cooked to desired degree of doneness. Serve at once.

POT ROAST
WITH VEGETABLES
6 to 8 servings

2 tablespoons fat
4- to 5-pound boneless beef pot roast

1½ teaspoons salt
¼ teaspoon pepper
1 large onion peeled, sliced
6 medium carrots scraped, cut in half
4 medium potatoes peeled, cut in half
¾ cup sliced celery

Preheat Sunbeam Cooker and Deep Fryer to 360°. Melt fat and brown pot roast on all sides. Add ¼ cup water. Season with salt and pepper. Turn Dial to E in Simmer; add onion. Cover and cook until meat is tender, 2½ to 3 hours. About 45 minutes before meat is done, add carrots, potatoes and celery. Set Dial at 320° until mixture comes to a boil; reduce heat again to Simmer. Cover and finish cooking. If desired, remove meat and vegetables, add 1½ cups of water to pan and thicken gravy.

BRAISED STUFFED
FLANK STEAK
6 servings

1½ pounds flank steak
Fresh bread
¼ cup minced onion
1 tablespoon snipped parsley
½ teaspoon celery salt
½ teaspoon dried sage
1 tablespoon butter or margarine
1 tablespoon salad oil
½ teaspoon peppercorns
1 teaspoon wine vinegar
1 beef bouillon cube
¼ cup flour

Have butcher score one side of steak in a diamond pattern. Tear a slice of fresh bread into pieces and put into Sunbeam Blender. Cover and process at Crumb. Empty into a measuring cup. Repeat process until 2 cups of crumbs are made. Empty into a mixing bowl. Add onion, parsley, salt and sage. Spread mixture over top of steak. Dot with butter. Roll up jelly-roll fashion and secure with skewers or string. Preheat Multi-Cooker Frypan to 360°. Heat salad oil in hot Frypan. Add steak and brown well on all sides. Add 1 cup hot water, peppercorns and vinegar. Cover, reduce heat to Simmer and cook 2 hours or until fork-tender. Remove steak and place on a heated serving platter. Remove peppercorns from sauce. Stir in 1 cup hot water and bouillon cube; bring to a boil at 300°. Mix flour and ¼ cup cold water to form a smooth paste. Stir into liquid in Frypan and cook until thickened. Season to taste if necessary and serve with slices of steak.

BEEF ROULADES WITH ROQUEFORT
6 servings

6 cubed beefsteaks, about
    1½ pounds
1 teaspoon salt
¼ teaspoon pepper
½ cup crumbled Roquefort
    cheese, packed
1 can (3 ounces) mushroom
    pieces
1 tablespoon minced onion
2 tablespoons flour
2 tablespoons shortening
1 can (12 ounces) vegetable
    juice cocktail
1 tablespoon Worcestershire
    sauce

Sprinkle steaks with half of the salt, pepper and Roquefort. Drain mushrooms, reserving juice. Combine mushrooms, onion and remaining salt and pepper. Divide mixture over Roquefort on steaks. Roll up steaks and fasten securely with wooden picks or tie with string. Dredge rolls in flour. Preheat Multi-Cooker Frypan to 340°. Melt shortening in hot Frypan and brown rolls well on all sides. Pour off as much fat as possible from Frypan. Combine juice drained from mushrooms, vegetable juice cocktail and Worcestershire. Pour mixture around beef. Cover Frypan, reduce heat to Simmer and cook 40 minutes to 1 hour or until tender. Remove roulades to a heated platter. Remove picks or strings. Stir remaining Roquefort into drippings in Frypan. Cook, stirring to bring up browned bits from bottom of pan. Pour sauce over roulades.

PEPPER STEAK
6 servings

3 pounds boneless sirloin steak
3 tablespoons whole peppercorns
1 tablespoon salad oil
2 tablespoons butter or
margarine,
½ cup dry red wine
2 tablespoons brandy
1 teaspoon salt

Wipe steak with a damp paper towel. Place peppercorns on a board and crush with a rolling pin. Pat crushed peppercorns into both sides of steak so that they stick to the meat. Preheat Multi-Cooker Frypan to 420°. Add oil and 1 tablespoon of the butter. When foam begins to subside, add steak and brown on both sides, about 2 minutes. Turn Dial to 360° and cook about 6 minutes on each side for medium rare, or cook to your own taste. Remove steak to a hot serving platter to keep warm. Add remaining butter, wine, brandy and salt to Frypan. Simmer, stirring until mixture comes just to a boil. Pour sauce over steak.

SAVORY STEAKS
ON TOAST
6 servings

¼ cup vegetable oil
2 cloves garlic, minced

½ teaspoon rosemary
½ teaspoon dry mustard
2 teaspoons soy sauce
¼ cup light corn syrup
6 cube steaks
Bread slices

Heat Multi-Cooker Frypan to 300°. Add oil. Sauté garlic in oil. Stir in next 4 ingredients. Place steaks in shallow dish and pour oil mixture over; marinate about 45 minutes. With Frypan set at 380°, brown steaks quickly on both sides. Remove steaks. Return marinade to Frypan and heat rapidly. Toast bread in Sunbeam Toaster. Serve steaks on toast, with a little heated marinade spooned over each.

HUNGARIAN HUNTERS'
STEW
4 to 6 servings

6 slices bacon, diced
1 cup minced onion
1 clove garlic, minced
1 cup sliced carrots
¼ cup red wine vinegar
3 cups beef stock or bouillon
2½ pounds boneless beef for
stew, cubed
Salt, pepper
¾ cup uncooked rice
1 green pepper, sliced

Put bacon in bottom of Cooker and Deep Fryer; turn Dial to 325° and cook until bacon has rendered most of its fat. Remove bacon and reserve. Pour all but a thin film of fat out of Cooker.

Recipe books for new Blenders and Mixers
contain information on speed settings for
other models in front, Instruction Section.

37

Sauté onions, stirring occasionally until limp. Add garlic and carrots; sauté briefly. Return reserved bacon to Cooker and Deep Fryer. Stir in vinegar, 2 cups beef stock, beef cubes. Season lightly with salt and pepper. Bring mixture to a boil, turn Cooker Dial down to first M of Simmer. Cover and cook 2 hours or until beef is nearly tender. Turn heat up to 300°. Stir in rice, pepper, remaining stock. Bring to a boil; turn down to R of Simmer; cover and cook 20 to 25 minutes or until rice is cooked. Add more stock, if necessary. Taste, adjust seasoning.

CARPETBAG STEAK
4 to 6 servings

2½ pounds boneless sirloin,
1½ inches thick
1 teaspoon salt
¼ teaspoon pepper
1½ dozen oysters
2 tablespoons cooking oil
1 tablespoon finely chopped
onion
2 teaspoons lemon juice
½ teaspoon paprika
1 tablespoon parsley
2 tablespoons sherry

Trim surplus fat from steak. With a sharp knife, cutting through the side of the steak, make a large pocket. Season pocket with salt and pepper. Fill pocket with oysters and fasten with skewers or sew with coarse

thread. Combine oil, onion, lemon juice and paprika. Place steak in shallow dish and pour oil mixture over. Marinate at least 1 hour, turning occasionally. Preheat Multi-Cooker Frypan to 380° and grease lightly. Place steak in Frypan and cook 6 to 7 minutes per side for rare, 8 to 10 for medium rare, turning once without piercing meat. Remove steak from Frypan; keep warm. Pour marinade into Frypan; bring to a boil. Stir in parsley and sherry and pour over steak.

CITRUS SWISS STEAK
4 servings

¼ cup flour
1 teaspoon salt
¼ teaspoon pepper
2 pounds round steak, 1½
inches thick
3 tablespoons shortening
2 medium onions, sliced
1 tablespoon brown sugar
1 cup grapefruit juice

Season flour with salt and pepper. Place steak on a board and pound half of flour mixture into each side. Reserve any leftover flour. Cut meat into 4 servings. Preheat Sunbeam Cooker and Deep Fryer to 350°. Melt shortening and brown meat on all sides. Remove meat. Add onions, brown lightly. Make a paste of reserved flour, brown sugar and a small part of grapefruit juice.

38

Stir into onions; gradually stir in remaining grapefruit juice. Return steak to Cooker. Turn Dial to first M in Simmer; cover and cook 1½ hours or until steak is tender.

Serving style: This goes particularly well with broad noodles, buttered and sprinkled with poppy seeds.

BEEF AND BEER
6 servings

2 pounds onions
Butter or margarine
3 pounds chuck or round steak, cut into cubes
Flour
Salt, pepper
3 cloves garlic
1 cup beer

Peel onions. Slice with Sunbeam Knife. Preheat Sunbeam Cooker and Deep Fryer to 300°. Melt 4 tablespoons butter in Cooker. Add onions and cook until soft and lightly browned. Remove onions. Dust meat cubes with a little flour. Melt 4 tablespoons butter in Cooker. Add meat and brown. Return onions to Cooker. Season with salt and pepper. Add garlic and beer. Bring to a boil. Reduce heat to Simmer. Cover and cook about 1¼ hours or until meat is tender.

CHICKEN-FRIED STEAK
4 servings

3 tablespoons flour
½ teaspoon salt
¼ teaspoon pepper
1 pound round steak, ¾ inch thick
2 tablespoons shortening
½ cup milk

Combine flour, salt and pepper. Pound this mixture into both sides of meat. Preheat Multi-Cooker Frypan to 350°. Melt shortening; brown meat on both sides. Lower heat to 260° and cook 10 minutes longer, turning occasionally. Remove steak to hot platter. Add milk to skillet slowly, stirring constantly. Cook until slightly thickened; pour over steak.

BEEF ROULADES
8 servings

2½ pounds round steak, cut ⅛ inch thick
¾ pound ground pork
1 teaspoon poultry seasoning
¾ teaspoon salt
½ clove garlic, crushed
2 tablespoons minced onion
¼ cup soft bread crumbs
8 slices bacon
3 tablespoons butter or margarine
8 small onions, peeled
⅓ cup flour

1 can (10 ounces) beef
bouillon
2½ cups dry red wine
1 pound fresh mushrooms
1 bay leaf

Cut round steak into 8 equal-sized pieces. Combine ground pork, poultry seasoning, salt, garlic, onion and bread crumbs. Toss lightly. Place about 2 tablespoons of mixture on each piece of beef. Roll up. Wrap each with a slice of bacon and tie with heavy thread. Preheat Multi-Cooker Frypan to 360°. Melt butter in hot Frypan. Add beef rolls and brown on all sides. Remove meat from Frypan. Add onions and brown lightly. Remove onions. Stir flour into Frypan. Gradually stir in bouillon and wine. Lower heat to 300° and cook, stirring constantly until mixture comes to a boil. Return meat and onions to Frypan. Add mushrooms and bay leaf. Simmer, covered, about 1 hour or until meat is tender. If sauce gets too thick during cooking time, thin with a little more red wine. Before serving, remove bay leaf and thread from beef rolls. Serve with onions, mushrooms and gravy from pan.

SWEDISH MEATBALLS
6 to 8 servings

2 cups fresh bread cubes
½ cup milk
¼ cup butter or margarine

1 onion, finely minced
3 eggs, beaten
1 teaspoon salt
¼ teaspoon pepper
2 teaspoons paprika
2 teaspoons ground nutmeg
1 teaspoon dry mustard
1½ pounds ground beef
1 teaspoon mixed herbs
1 clove garlic, minced
2 cups beef bouillon
2 teaspoons bitters
1 beef bouillon cube
2 teaspoons tomato paste
¼ cup flour
2 cups sour cream

Combine bread cubes and milk and let stand. Preheat Multi-Cooker Frypan to 300°. Melt 1 tablespoon of the butter in Frypan. Cook onion until tender but not browned. Squeeze as much of the milk out of the bread as possible and place bread in a mixing bowl. Add the cooked onion, eggs, salt, pepper, paprika, nutmeg and mustard. Blend well. Add beef and mixed herbs. Blend lightly but thoroughly with your hands until well mixed. Turn Frypan to 320°. Shape mixture into balls 1 inch in diameter. Heat remaining 3 tablespoons butter in Frypan. Brown meatballs well on all sides in hot butter. Remove meatballs from pan. Cook garlic in pan drippings 1 minute. Combine beef bouillon, bitters, bouillon cube, tomato paste and flour. Stir well. Cook, stirring until mixture thickens and comes to a boil. Stir in sour cream and heat, but *do not boil*. Return meatballs to pan and let simmer at very low temperature until well heated.

HAMBURGER ORIENTAL STYLE
4 to 5 servings

1 pound ground beef
2 cups diagonally sliced celery
1 envelope (1⅜ ounces) onion soup mix
1 tablespoon cornstarch
1 can (1 pound) bean sprouts, drained
2 teaspoons soy sauce
Chinese noodles

Preheat Multi-Cooker Frypan to 420°. Put ground beef and celery in Frypan and cook, stirring with a fork until meat is broken up and has lost its red color. Add remaining ingredients except noodles. Add 2 cups water; bring to a boil, stirring constantly. Cover, lower heat to Simmer and cook about 10 minutes or just until celery is still crisply tender. Stir occasionally. Serve over noodles.

PORCUPINE MEATBALLS
6 servings

1½ pounds ground beef
½ cup uncooked rice
1 tablespoon minced onion
½ teaspoon allspice

1 teaspoon salt
¼ teaspoon pepper
1 can (10½ ounces) condensed tomato soup

Combine ground beef, rice, onion, allspice, salt and pepper. Blend lightly but thoroughly. Shape into small balls about 1½ inches in diameter. Combine tomato soup and ½ cup water in Multi-Cooker Frypan. Turn Dial to 300° and bring to a boil. Drop meatballs into liquid. Lower heat to Simmer and cover. Cook gently about 2 hours. During cooking time, stir occasionally and add more water if needed.

HUNGARIAN GOULASH
4 servings

¼ cup cooking oil
1 large Spanish onion, chopped
2 pounds beef chuck, cut into 1½-inch cubes
¾ cup hot beef stock or bouillon
2 teaspoons paprika
Salt, pepper
1 cup diced raw potatoes
1 cup diced raw carrots
¼ cup tomato juice
1 package (8 ounces) wide egg noodles

Heat the cooking oil in Multi-Cooker Frypan to 350°. Sauté the onion until soft and transparent, but not browned. Add beef cubes and brown. Add stock, paprika, salt and pepper to taste. Cover, reduce heat to 250° and simmer 1 hour. Add potatoes, carrots and tomato juice; simmer 30 minutes longer or until beef is tender and vegetables cooked. Meanwhile, cook noodles according to package directions. Serve goulash over noodles.

Try it this way: Omit tomato juice. When beef is tender and vegetables cooked, stir in ½ cup sour cream. Heat through, but *do not boil.* Correct seasoning.

SOUTH SEAS BEEF
4 servings

1 pound ground round
2 tablespoons cooking oil
½ cup sliced water chestnuts
2 cans (3 ounces each) sliced
mushrooms with liquid
½ cup white raisins
½ cup beef bouillon
1 teaspoon curry powder
1 tablespoon soy sauce
1 package (10 ounces)
frozen peas
1 unpeeled orange, cut into 6
slices
½ cup salted cashew nuts

Heat Multi-Cooker Frypan to 340°. Brown beef in oil. Add water chestnuts, mushrooms, raisins, bouillon, curry powder, soy sauce and peas, breaking up peas with a fork. Stir to blend. Top with orange slices. Turn Dial to Simmer. Cover and cook 15 minutes. Toss in cashew nuts.

BROILED STEAK
4 to 6 servings

1 large steak, porterhouse,
T-bone or sirloin, 1½ inches
thick
Salt, pepper

Place rack in low position in Sunbeam Broiler Cover Frypan. Preheat at 420° until element is red. Trim excess fat off steak and slash edge in several places to prevent curling. Place steak on rack. Cover; open vent. Broil to degree of doneness desired. Season. For rare, broil 10 minutes first side, 8 minutes after turning; for medium, broil 12 minutes first side, 10 minutes after turning; for well done, broil 15 minutes first side, 13 minutes after turning.

BURGUNDY BURGERS
4 servings

1 pound ground chuck
½ cup dry Burgundy, divided
1 teaspoon salt
⅛ teaspoon pepper
2 tablespoons butter or
margarine
2 tablespoons snipped parsley
2 tablespoons snipped chives

Combine chuck, ¼ cup Burgundy, salt and pepper. Mix lightly. Shape into 4 patties. Preheat Multi-Cooker Frypan to 360°. Heat butter in Frypan. Fry

patties on both sides to the desired degree of doneness. Remove patties to a warm serving platter. Pour off all fat from Frypan. Add remaining wine, parsley and chives. Cook at 300° about 1 minute, stirring up browned bits from bottom of Frypan. Pour sauce over patties and serve hot.

BURGER STROGANOFF
4 to 6 servings

½ cup minced onion
¼ cup butter or margarine
1 pound ground beef
1 clove garlic, minced
2 teaspoons salt
¼ teaspoon pepper
1 pound mushrooms, sliced
2 tablespoons flour
1 cup sour cream

Preheat Multi-Cooker Frypan to 340°. Cook onion in hot butter in Frypan about 3 minutes, stirring occasionally. Add beef, garlic, salt, pepper and mushrooms. Cook, stirring with a fork until meat is broken up and has lost its red color. Sprinkle flour over top of meat mixture and cook, stirring constantly, 2 minutes. Lower heat to Simmer. Add sour cream and heat thoroughly, but *do not boil.*

Serving style: Serve over hot cooked noodles, rice or mashed potatoes.

BARBECUED MEAT LOAF
12 servings

¼ cup molasses
¼ cup prepared mustard
¼ cup vinegar
1 can (8 ounces) tomato sauce
2 eggs
3 cups soft bread
1 medium onion, quartered
8 sprigs parsley
1 tablespoon salt
½ teaspoon thyme
3 pounds ground beef

Combine molasses, mustard and vinegar in a small bowl. Add ½ cup of this mixture to the tomato sauce and eggs in a large mixing bowl. Beat with Mixmaster Hand Mixer, or Mixmaster Mixer, until well blended. Tear a slice of fresh bread into pieces and put into Sunbeam Blender. Cover and process at Crumb. Empty bread crumbs into a measuring cup. Repeat process until 3 cups have been made. Put into mixing bowl with tomato mixture. Place onion and parsley in Blender. Cover and process at Chop. Put into the mixing bowl. Add salt, thyme and ground beef. Mix well. Form into a loaf in a shallow baking pan. Brush with part of the remaining molasses mixture. Bake in a preheated 350°F. oven 1½ hours, brushing with remaining mixture.

SPAGHETTI WITH MEATBALLS
4 servings

1 pound ground beef
1 teaspoon salt
⅛ teaspoon pepper
2 tablespoons olive oil
½ cup minced onion
1 clove garlic, minced
2 cans (8 ounces each) tomato sauce
¼ teaspoon Tabasco sauce
Hot cooked spaghetti
Grated Parmesan cheese

Sprinkle beef with salt and pepper and form into balls. Preheat Multi-Cooker Frypan to 320°. Heat oil in Frypan. Brown meatballs on all sides in hot oil. Add onions and garlic. Stir and cook just a few minutes. Add tomato sauce and Tabasco. Cover, reduce heat to Simmer and cook 20 to 30 minutes. Serve with hot cooked spaghetti and grated Parmesan cheese.

SPAGHETTI SAUCE
4 to 6 servings

1 tablespoon salad oil
2 onions, coarsely chopped
3 cloves garlic, minced
½ pound ground chuck
1 can (2 pounds 3 ounces) Italian plum tomatoes
1 can (6 ounces) tomato paste
1 teaspoon salt

1 teaspoon oregano
¼ teaspoon basil
¼ teaspoon freshly ground black pepper
1 sprig parsley
½ cup grated Parmesan cheese

Heat oil in Sunbeam Cooker and Deep Fryer with Dial set at 300°. Add onion and garlic and cook 2 minutes, stirring constantly. Add beef and fry until beef is lightly browned. Add remaining ingredients. Bring to a boil, then turn Dial to Simmer. Cover and simmer about 2 hours or until sauce is well blended and slightly thickened. Serve over hot cooked spaghetti.

MUSHROOM WINE BURGERS
3 or 4 servings

1 pound ground chuck
¼ cup light cream
¼ cup milk
1 tablespoon minced onion
1 teaspoon salt
¼ teaspoon pepper
2 tablespoons butter or margarine
2 tablespoons flour
½ cup beef bouillon
½ cup red wine
1 teaspoon Worcestershire sauce
2 tablespoons chopped parsley
1 can (4 ounces) sliced mushrooms
Salt, pepper
3 or 4 slices bread

Combine chuck, cream, milk, onion, salt and pepper. Toss

Recipe books for new Blenders and Mixers contain information on speed settings for other models in front, Instruction Section.

45

lightly with a fork. Shape into 3 or 4 thick patties. Preheat Multi-Cooker Frypan to 380°. Melt butter. Add patties and fry just until browned on both sides. Remove patties and keep warm. Turn heat down to 300°. Add flour to the drippings. Stir in bouillon and red wine. Cook, stirring constantly until mixture boils and thickens. Add Worcestershire, parsley and mushrooms with liquid. Season to taste with salt and pepper. Return patties to sauce and simmer until meat is cooked to the desired degree of doneness. Make toast from bread slices in Sunbeam Toaster. Place meat patties on toast and pour sauce over top.

GLORIOUS LIVER
4 servings

1 pound calves' liver
Flour
Salt, pepper
Paprika
2 tablespoons butter
2 tablespoons salad oil
1 clove garlic, minced
½ cup dry white wine
2 tablespoons snipped parsley
¾ cup sour cream

Cut liver into thin strips about ½ inch thick. Dredge with flour seasoned with salt, pepper and paprika. Preheat Multi-Cooker Frypan to 340°. Add butter and oil, and heat. Add strips of liver and garlic and cook very quickly,

turning so that all the liver strips become browned and cooked. This should take about 2 to 4 minutes. Remove liver to a hot platter and keep warm. Pour off most of fat from Frypan. Add wine and parsley and cook, stirring, so that browned bits are brought up from bottom of pan. Add sour cream and heat, but *do not boil.* Taste and add more seasoning if necessary. Return liver strips to pan and heat and stir. Serve immediately over buttered noodles or hot cooked rice.

CREOLE LIVER
4 servings

3 slices lean bacon
2 tablespoons flour
½ teaspoon salt
¼ teaspoon pepper
1 pound thin-sliced beef liver
1 cup vegetable-juice cocktail
1 medium onion, thinly sliced

Place bacon slices in Multi-Cooker Frypan. Turn Dial to 340° and cook bacon until crisp. Remove and reserve. Combine flour, salt and pepper and use for dredging liver slices. Brown liver in a small amount of bacon fat. Add vegetable-juice cocktail, onion and crumbled bacon. Turn Frypan to Simmer and cook, covered, 10 minutes or so until liver is tender.

46

PERFECT POULTRY

Chicken is everybody's favorite, young and old alike. Here are new and inventive ways with poultry—both fancy and down-to-earth—as well as new approaches to old standbys. Your Multi-Cooker Frypan, Cooker and Deep Fryer and Sunbeam Knife will all see good service here—bring Frypan and Cooker to the table for piping hot dishing-up and second helpings.

CHICKEN FRICASSEE
6 servings

3½- to 4-pound stewing chicken, cut up
Flour
3 tablespoons fat
2 teaspoons salt
⅛ teaspoon pepper
½ teaspoon poultry seasoning
1½ cups diluted canned condensed cream of chicken soup
1 large onion, diced
½ cup celery, diced
1 can (4 ounces) sliced mushrooms

Dip cut up chicken in flour. Preheat Multi-Cooker Frypan to 360°. Add fat. Brown chicken, turning as necessary and removing browned pieces. When all is browned, spoon off fat. Place chicken in Frypan meaty side down and sprinkle with salt, pepper and poultry seasoning. Add soup slowly, together with the remaining ingredients. When liquid is boiling, turn Dial to 220°. Cover; simmer 3 to 4 hours until larger pieces are tender. Add more seasoning and a few drops of yellow food coloring if desired.

CHICKEN BREASTS WITH MUSHROOMS
4 servings

½ cup olive oil
1 small onion, finely chopped
1 clove garlic, finely chopped
2 large chicken breasts, cut in half
½ pound mushrooms, thinly sliced
1 cup dry white wine
Salt, white pepper to taste

Preheat Multi-Cooker Frypan to 340°. Heat olive oil. Sauté onion and garlic until lightly browned. Add chicken and sauté until lightly browned on both sides. Reduce heat to Simmer. Add remaining ingredients. Cover and cook at Simmer 25 to 30 minutes or until chicken is tender.

CHICKEN TARRAGON
4 servings

1 broiler-fryer, cut into serving pieces
1 tablespoon seasoned salt
½ teaspoon freshly ground black pepper
Dash paprika
¼ cup butter or margarine
1 medium onion, thinly sliced
½ pound fresh mushrooms, sliced
1 teaspoon tarragon

Preheat Multi-Cooker Frypan to 340°. Sprinkle chicken pieces with blended salt, pepper and paprika. Melt butter in heated Frypan. Add chicken pieces and brown on all sides. Remove chicken. Add onion and mushrooms and cook until just tender but not browned. Return chicken to Frypan. Sprinkle with tarragon. Cover and reduce heat to Simmer. Cook 25 to 30 minutes or until chicken is tender.

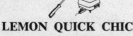

LEMON QUICK CHICK
4 to 6 servings

3 whole chicken breasts
¼ cup butter or margarine
1 tablespoon flour
½ teaspoon tarragon
½ teaspoon salt
1 chicken bouillon cube
1 whole lemon, thinly sliced

Have butcher bone and remove skin from chicken breasts. Cut each breast in half and cut each half into 10 or 12 strips with Sunbeam Knife. Preheat Multi-Cooker Frypan to 380°. Melt butter. Add chicken pieces. Sprinkle with flour, tarragon and salt. Cook 5 minutes, stirring constantly. Combine ¾ cup hot water and bouillon cube. Pour over chicken. Add lemon slices. Cover and reduce heat to Simmer. Cook 3 minutes.

Serving style: This quick-and-easy dish is made even better if served with hot cooked rice combined with 2 tablespoons chopped parsley.

CHICKEN
IN WHITE WINE
4 servings

2 whole chicken breasts
Flour
½ cup butter or margarine
½ teaspoon salt
Pepper, freshly ground
1 tablespoon tarragon
¾ cup dry white wine, divided
3 tablespoons snipped parsley

Have butcher split and bone chicken breasts. Place between 2 pieces of wax paper and pound as flat as possible with a pounder or the flat side of a heavy cleaver. Dust breasts lightly with flour. Preheat Multi-Cooker Frypan to 350°. Melt butter in Frypan. Add chicken breasts, and brown lightly on both sides. Add salt, pepper, tarragon and ½ cup of the wine. Reduce heat to Simmer and cook, uncovered, about 10 minutes or until chicken breasts are tender. Place chicken on a warm serving platter. Add parsley and remaining white wine. Turn Dial on Frypan to 380° and cook, stirring constantly until sauce is reduced a little. Taste and add salt and pepper if necessary. Pour sauce over chicken breasts.

continuing to stir. Drain pineapple, reserving syrup. Add drained pineapple, ½ cup reserved pineapple syrup, ¾ cup water, bouillon cube, onion and tarragon. Bring mixture to a boil. Reduce heat to a high Simmer, cover and cook 4 minutes. Blend cornstarch and 2 tablespoons cold water. Stir all at once into Frypan and cook at 360°, stirring rapidly until thickened. Add pimiento and serve immediately.

TRADE WINDS CHICKEN
6 servings

3 broiler-fryer chicken breasts
¼ cup butter or margarine
1 teaspoon salt
1 green pepper, cut into strips
1 cup diagonally sliced celery
1 can (20½ ounces) pineapple
    chunks
1 chicken bouillon cube
2 tablespoons instant minced
    onion
1 teaspoon dried leaf tarragon
2 tablespoons cornstarch
1 can (4 ounces) pimiento,
    drained, cut in half

Have butcher bone and skin chicken breasts. With Sunbeam Knife, cut each breast half into 10 or 12 strips. Preheat Multi-Cooker Frypan to 420°. Melt butter in hot Frypan. Add strips of chicken and sprinkle with salt. Cook, stirring constantly, 3 minutes. Add green pepper and celery and cook 2 minutes longer,

CHICKEN WITH
PEA PODS
8 servings

4 whole chicken breasts
2½ teaspoons salt
¼ cup cooking oil
1 can (1 pound 4 ounces)
pineapple chunks in unsweetened
    juice
2 cans (8 ounces each) water
chestnuts, drained and thinly
    sliced
¼ cup soy sauce
½ cup molasses
2 chicken bouillon cubes
1 package (7 ounces) frozen
    snow peas
¼ cup cornstarch
4 cups hot cooked rice

Have butcher skin and bone chicken breasts. With Sunbeam Knife cut each breast in half and each half into 10 to 12 strips. Sprinkle chicken strips with 2 teaspoons salt. Preheat Multi-Cooker Frypan to 380°. Heat oil in hot Frypan. Add chicken, cook, stirring about 3 minutes or until chicken turns white. Drain pineapple, reserving chunks. Add pineapple juice, water chestnuts, soy sauce, molasses, 1 cup water and bouillon cubes to chicken. Mix well. Cover, reduce heat to Simmer and cook 5 to 10 minutes or until chicken is tender. Add reserved pineapple chunks, snow peas and remaining ½ teaspoon salt. Cover and simmer 2 more minutes, stirring occasionally. Combine cornstarch and ½ cup cold water to make a smooth paste. Stir into chicken mixture and cook, stirring until sauce is clear and thickened. Serve with hot cooked rice.

QUICK CHICKEN STROGANOFF
4 servings

2 whole broiler-fryer chicken breasts
3 tablespoons butter or margarine
2 tablespoons finely chopped scallions
½ teaspoon salt
1 can (10½ ounces) condensed cream of mushroom soup, undiluted
1 can (3 ounces) sliced mushrooms
½ cup sour cream
Hot cooked noodles

Have butcher bone and remove skins from chicken breasts. Cut each breast in half with Sunbeam Knife and cut each half into 10 or 12 strips. Preheat Multi-Cooker Frypan to 380°. Melt butter in hot Frypan. Add chicken and scallions, sprinkle with salt. Cook 6 minutes, stirring occasionally. Add mushroom soup, sliced mushrooms with liquid and ¼ cup water. Heat to boiling, stirring until mixture is smooth. Reduce heat to Simmer. Blend in sour cream and heat, but *do not boil*. Serve over hot cooked noodles.

QUICK CHICKEN A LA KING
6 servings

3 whole broiler-fryer chicken breasts
¼ cup butter or margarine
¼ cup chopped onion
1 can (10¾ ounces) cream of mushroom soup
½ soup can milk
2 tablespoons chopped pimiento
Hot waffles

Have butcher bone and remove skin from chicken breasts. Cut chicken into strips with Sunbeam Knife. Preheat Multi-Cooker Frypan to 380°. Add butter. When butter is hot, add strips of chicken and onion. Cook, stirring constantly, 5 minutes. Add soup, milk and pimiento. Cover and simmer 3 minutes or until thoroughly heated. Bake waffles (page 105). Serve chicken over waffles.

CHICKEN MAXIMILIAN
8 servings

2 broiler-fryer chickens, cut into
quarters
1½ teaspoons salt
1 teaspoon paprika
¼ cup butter or margarine
2 tablespoons slivered orange
rind
1½ cups orange juice
2 teaspoons instant minced onion
½ teaspoon ginger
½ teaspoon dried tarragon
4 teaspoons cornstarch
1 avocado

Sprinkle chicken quarters on
both sides with salt and paprika.
Preheat Multi-Cooker Frypan to
340°. Add butter. Add chicken
quarters, a few at a time, and
brown well on both sides. Remove chicken quarters as they
are browned. Return chicken to
Frypan. Add orange rind, orange
juice, onion, ginger and tarragon.
Cover. Reduce heat to Simmer
and cook 30 minutes or until
chicken is tender. Remove
chicken and place on a heated
platter. Blend cornstarch with a
little cold water to make a
smooth paste. Stir into sauce in
Frypan. Cook, stirring constantly
until mixture thickens and comes
to a boil. Peel avocado; cut into
wedges. Arrange avocado around
chicken on platter. Pour a small
amount of sauce over chicken.
Pass remaining sauce.

SWEET AND PUNGENT TURKEY
4 to 6 servings

1 egg
½ teaspoon soy sauce
3 cups large cooked turkey
chunks
Cooking oil for frying
½ cup cornstarch
2 tablespoons butter or
margarine
1 clove garlic, crushed
1 bunch scallions, cut into 1-inch
pieces
2 onions, cut into wedges
1 can (13¼ ounces) pineapple
chunks
1 cup sugar
1 cup cider vinegar
2 tablespoons cornstarch
1 package (7 ounces) frozen
Chinese pea pods
2 tablespoons ketchup
2 teaspoons soy sauce
Hot cooked rice

Beat egg with ½ teaspoon soy
sauce in a shallow bowl. Add
turkey chunks and toss well. Let
stand about 10 minutes. Heat oil
in Sunbeam Cooker and Deep
Fryer set at 375°. Put cornstarch
in a small plastic bag. Shake turkey pieces, a few at a time, in
cornstarch until evenly coated.
Drop turkey pieces into hot fat.
Fry, turning once, 3 to 5 minutes or until golden on all sides.
Lift up basket to drain. Turn out
on paper towels. Keep warm in

a 200°F. oven while preparing sauce. Preheat Multi-Cooker Frypan at 300°. Melt butter in Frypan. Add garlic, scallions and onion wedges and cook about 5 minutes or until golden. Drain pineapple liquid into a 1-cup measure. Add water to make 1 cup liquid. Reserve pineapple chunks. Add pineapple liquid, sugar and vinegar to onions in Frypan. Cook, stirring, about 2 minutes. Combine cornstarch with ¼ cup water in a small bowl to make a smooth paste. Stir into liquid in Frypan. Bring to a boil, stirring constantly. Add pea pods, ketchup and soy sauce and simmer 5 minutes. Add turkey pieces and pineapple chunks and stir very gently. Heat thoroughly. Serve with rice.

CHICKEN CACCIATORE
4 servings

2½-pound broiler-fryer, cut up
¼ cup flour
¼ cup cooking oil
1 medium onion, coarsely
    chopped
1 medium green pepper, coarsely
    chopped
1 clove garlic, minced
1¼ teaspoons salt
⅛ teaspoon pepper
2 bay leaves
1 can (16 ounces) tomatoes
1 can (8 ounces) tomato sauce
¼ cup dry white wine
2 tablespoons chopped parsley

Coat chicken pieces with flour. Preheat Multi-Cooker Frypan to 340°. Heat oil in Frypan. Add chicken and cook until lightly browned, turning as needed. Remove chicken. Add onion, green pepper and garlic; cook about 3 minutes. Add chicken. Add seasonings, tomatoes, tomato sauce and wine. Cover, reduce heat to Simmer and cook 30 minutes or until chicken is tender. Turn chicken occasionally during cooking time. Add parsley and serve.

CHICKEN HUNGARIAN
6 to 8 servings

½ cup flour
2 tablespoons hot paprika (or 1
    tablespoon paprika plus 1
    teaspoon cayenne pepper)
1 teaspoon salt
½ teaspoon pepper
¼ teaspoon oregano
2 2½- to 3-pound broiler-fryers,
    cut into serving pieces
⅓ cup cooking oil
1 cup chopped onions
1 cup sliced mushrooms
1 cup dry white wine
3 chicken bouillon cubes
2 cups sour cream

Combine flour, paprika, salt, pepper and oregano in a large paper bag. Add a few chicken pieces and shake to coat evenly. Repeat with remaining chicken pieces. Preheat Multi-Cooker Frypan to 340°. Heat oil and cook chicken

pieces, browning on all sides, about 15 minutes. Fry in two batches, if necessary. Remove chicken. Reduce heat to 300°. Add onion and mushrooms. Sauté until just golden. Add wine and bouillon cubes and stir until bouillon cubes are dissolved. Return chicken to Frypan. Cover and reduce heat to Simmer. Cook until chicken is tender, about 40 minutes. Remove chicken and place on a hot serving platter. Stir sour cream into drippings in pan. Heat thoroughly, but *do not boil.* Pour over chicken. Serve with hot cooked rice or noodles if desired.

CHICKEN KIEV
8 rolls or 4 servings

½ cup butter or margarine
1 clove garlic, crushed
2 teaspoons snipped chives
2 teaspoons snipped parsley
½ teaspoon salt
⅛ teaspoon pepper
4 whole chicken breasts, skinned and boned
1 cup cornstarch
1 cup flour
1 egg
Fat for frying

In a small bowl combine butter, garlic, chives, parsley, salt and pepper. Blend thoroughly. Place butter on a sheet of wax paper. Pat out into a roll about ½ inch thick. Wrap in wax paper and freeze until very firm. Cut each

breast in half. Place each piece between two sheets of wax paper and pound with a rolling pin to ¼-inch thickness. Divide butter mixture into 8 pieces. Lay one piece on each half of chicken breast. Roll it up firmly in the chicken, tucking in the sides. Secure with toothpicks or tie with string. Place in refrigerator. In a bowl combine cornstarch, flour, 1 cup water and egg. Beat with Mixmaster Hand Mixer at medium speed until very smooth. Preheat fat in Sunbeam Cooker and Deep Fryer to 375°F. Dip rolls, one at a time, into batter, drain slightly and fry 4 at a time 10 minutes or until golden brown. Lift up basket and drain. Turn out on paper towels to drain. Repeat. Serve immediately.

CHICKEN MARENGO
4 servings

2½-pound broiler-fryer, cut up
½ teaspoon salt
¼ teaspoon pepper
¼ cup flour
⅓ cup cooking oil
2 onions, thinly sliced
1 clove garlic
¼ pound mushrooms, sliced
3 tablespoons flour
1 can (1 pound 4 ounces) tomatoes
¼ cup sherry

Sprinkle chicken with salt and pepper. Lightly coat with flour. Preheat Multi-Cooker Frypan to

340°. Heat cooking oil. Add chicken pieces and brown lightly on all sides. Remove chicken and place in a 2-quart casserole. Add onion, garlic and mushrooms to oil in Frypan and cook until tender. Remove garlic clove. Add flour and mix well. Add tomatoes and ½ cup water and cook, stirring constantly until mixture comes to a boil and is slightly thickened. Add sherry. Pour mixture over chicken in casserole. Cover and bake about 45 minutes in a preheated 350°F. oven or until chicken is tender.

FLAMING BREAST OF CHICKEN
8 servings

4 large chicken breasts
¾ cup flour
2 teaspoons salt
¼ teaspoon pepper
½ teaspoon crushed oregano or poultry seasoning
¼ pound butter or margarine
Seasoned salt
1 small bunch scallions, sliced crosswise with part of tops
½ pound fresh mushrooms or 1 can (4 ounces) stems and pieces, drained
5 ounces apricot or peach brandy
2 egg yolks
3 cups milk
1 cup half-and-half

Remove center bone from chicken breasts and cut breasts in half.

Combine flour, salt, pepper and oregano. Dip chicken pieces into mixture, coating well; shake off excess and reserve flour mixture. Preheat Multi-Cooker Frypan to 340°. Add butter. When melted, brown chicken breasts, 4 halves at a time, turning as necessary. When all are browned return to Frypan. Sprinkle chicken with seasoned salt. Cover; open vent. Set Dial to R of Simmer and cook about 30 minutes or until chicken is tender. Turn pieces after 15 minutes. Remove when tender and keep warm. Add scallions and sliced mushrooms to Frypan. Sauté at the R of Simmer. Add 1 ounce of the brandy. Stir with a wooden spoon, scraping bottom of pan to remove browned bits. Add 3 tablespoons of the remaining flour mixture and blend. Gradually add beaten egg yolks, which have been combined with the milk and half-and-half, stirring constantly until thickened. Taste and season further as desired. Return chicken to sauce, stacking in center of pan. Pour remaining brandy over chicken pieces; set aflame. Serve at once.

STEWED CHICKEN WITH DUMPLINGS
6 servings

4-pound stewing chicken, cut into serving pieces
1½ teaspoons salt

*1 medium-sized onion, cut in
half
1 carrot, cut into pieces
2 ribs celery, cut into pieces
2 sprigs parsley
3 or 4 peppercorns
½ bay leaf
1 whole clove*

Place chicken in Sunbeam Cooker and Deep Fryer, putting the back in first, then giblets, legs and wings, with breast on top. Add boiling water to cover chicken a little more than half—top pieces will steam-cook. Add vegetables and seasonings. Set Dial at 300°. When boiling point is reached, turn Dial to Simmer, and cover. Test for tenderness after 2 hours (white meat becomes tender first). Remove tender pieces, cover and continue cooking until remainder is tender. Total cooking time: about 3 to 4 hours.

DUMPLINGS

*2 cups sifted all-purpose flour
3 teaspoons baking powder
1 teaspoon salt
3 tablespoons shortening
1 cup milk*

Sift together flour, baking powder and salt. Blend in shortening with two knives until mixture looks like coarse meal. Add milk, mix quickly with a fork only until blended. Drop by tablespoonfuls onto chicken pieces. Slide dough off spoon with a rub-

ber spatula. Do not put dumplings into liquid, as this makes them soggy. Cook ten minutes, uncovered, with Dial set at Simmer so that liquid keeps bubbling. Cover. Simmer 10 minutes longer.

COUNTRY CAPTAIN
8 servings

*½ cup flour
3 teaspoons salt
½ teaspoon pepper
2 broiler-fryer chickens, cut
into serving pieces
1½ cups butter or margarine
2 medium green peppers,
chopped
2 medium onions, chopped
2 cloves garlic, minced
1 tablespoon curry powder
1 teaspoon dried thyme
2 cans (16 ounces each) tomatoes
⅓ cup currants or raisins*

Combine flour, salt and pepper in a bag. Shake chicken pieces, a few at a time, until they are coated with flour mixture. Preheat Multi-Cooker Frypan to 360°. Melt butter in hot Frypan. Add chicken and brown on both sides; remove from Frypan. Add green pepper, onions, garlic, curry powder and thyme to butter remaining in Frypan. Cook until onions and green pepper are tender but not brown. Return chicken pieces to Frypan. Add tomatoes and bring to a boil. Cover and simmer 15 minutes.

Uncover; add currants and simmer 15 minutes longer or until chicken pieces are tender.

CHICKEN ENCORE
4 servings

1 slice dry bread, broken into
pieces
2 slices fresh bread, broken into
pieces
2 cup diced cold chicken
1 cup diced celery
½ medium onion, quartered
1 egg
1 teaspoon salt
¼ teaspoon pepper
½ teaspoon sage
¼ cup butter or margarine,
melted

Grease baking pan. Crumb dry bread in Sunbeam Blender; set aside. Crumb fresh bread and empty into mixing bowl. Chop chicken in Blender, half at a time. Add to crumbs in bowl. Chop celery and onion, add to chicken. Put egg and seasonings into Blender; cover and process at Stir until well mixed. Add to other ingredients in bowl and mix well. Shape mixture into cylinders, brush with melted butter and roll in dry crumbs. Place in prepared pan, pour remaining butter over top, and bake 45 minutes in a preheated 375° F. oven.

FRIED CHICKEN

Frying chickens, cut into serving
pieces
Seasoned salt
Flour
Salt, pepper
Shortening for deep frying

Wash chicken, sprinkle with seasoned salt. Put flour, salt and pepper into a bag. Place several pieces of chicken into bag and shake until well coated. Fry in preheated shortening in Sunbeam Cooker and Deep Fryer, set at 350°. One whole chicken up to 3 pounds in weight may be fried at one time. Fill basket about half full, or slip one piece at a time into hot shortening with tongs. Fry until browned and tender, arranging larger, meaty pieces on bottom of basket, smaller pieces on top. Frying time will vary with size of chicken and quantity fried at one time. Test for tenderness by lifting basket to drain position. Pierce thickest part of drumstick with a sharp knife. It should cut easily and show no trace of pink color in juices.

CREAMY
CHICKEN OMELET
4 servings

6 eggs, separated
6 tablespoons milk

Recipe books for new Blenders and Mixers
contain information on speed settings for
other models in front, Instruction Section.

½ teaspoon salt
¼ teaspoon white pepper
2 tablespoons butter or
    margarine
1 cup diced cooked chicken
1 can (10¾ ounces) chicken
    gravy
Parsley, chopped

Place egg whites in large Mixmaster Mixer bowl. With Dial set at No. 12, beat until stiff. Place egg yolks in small Mixmaster Mixer bowl and beat until thick and lemon-colored. Turn Dial to No. 2 and add milk and seasonings. Fold yolk mixture into whites with Dial set at No. 1. Melt butter in 9-inch skillet. When hot, pour in egg mixture. Cook over low heat 3 to 5 minutes or until lightly browned on bottom. Run under broiler a few inches from heat and cook until omelet is set and top springs back when touched. Meanwhile heat chicken and gravy together. Slide omelet onto platter; top with chicken mixture. Sprinkle with parsley.

CHICKEN BREASTS BUFFET STYLE
6 to 8 serving

4 large chicken breasts
¾ cup flour
2 teaspoons salt
¼ teaspoon pepper
½ teaspon poultry seasoning
½ cup butter or margarine,
    divided

1 pound fresh mushrooms, sliced
2 tablespoons grated onion
1 pint light cream
¼ cup dry sherry
Paprika
1½ cups raw brown rice
3 cups cooked, buttered peas

Remove center bone from chicken breasts and cut breasts in half. Combine flour, salt, pepper and poultry seasoning. Dip chicken pieces into mixture, coating well; shake off excess. Preheat Multi-Cooker Frypan to 340°. Melt ⅔ of the butter. Add chicken and brown well. Cover; open vent. Set Dial to Simmer and cook about 30 minutes or until chicken is tender. Turn pieces after 15 minutes. Meanwhile, cook rice as directed on package. When done, pack into a well-buttered 8½-inch ring mold. Cover and keep warm. When chicken is tender, remove and keep warm. Add mushrooms, onion and remaining butter to Frypan. Turn Dial to 300°. Sauté, stirring gently until barely tender. Turn Dial to Simmer, add cream; stir and simmer for a few minutes. Stir in sherry very slowly. Turn Dial to Warm. Arrange chicken in Frypan and spoon sauce over it. Cover. Unmold rice on warm platter. Sprinkle with paprika. Place peas in center. Spoon mushroom sauce over rice servings.

FABULOUS FISH

Fish and shellfish make welcome main-dish changes from meat and poultry, both for family meals and when you're entertaining. And they're so good from the nutritional point of view as well! Your Sunbeam Appliances give you a hand both in cooking and serving—and you'll win praises from both family and guests for the delicious variety of the food that you serve.

FRIED FISH
6 servings

2 pounds fish fillets or steaks
¾ cup flour
2 teaspoons salt
¼ teaspoon pepper
1 egg
1 cup fine dry bread crumbs
Shortening or oil

Cut fish into serving pieces. Combine flour, salt and pepper. Beat together egg and ¼ cup water. Dip fish in seasoned flour, then in egg mixture and then in bread crumbs. Place fish on a piece of wax paper and let stand a few minutes. Fill Sunbeam Cooker and Deep Fryer at least half full with shortening or oil. Heat to 375°. Fry fish, a few pieces at a time, 3 to 6 minutes or until golden brown. Drain. Put on paper towels to drain thoroughly. Serve at once with desired sauce.

BATTER-DIPPED FISH
6 servings

2 eggs
⅔ cup milk
1 cup sifted all-purpose flour
1 teaspoon baking powder
½ teaspoon salt
2 tablespoons melted shortening
2 pounds fish fillets or steaks
Shortening or oil

Put eggs into small bowl of Mixmaster Mixer and beat at No. 6 1 minute. Add milk and beat at No. 3 1 minute. Sift together flour, baking powder and salt; add to milk mixture. Add shortening and beat at No. 1 until blended. Dip fish into batter. Allow to drain slightly. Fry in preheated shortening at 375° in Sunbeam Cooker and Deep Fryer about 5 to 6 minutes until browned, turning as necessary to brown on all sides. Drain on paper towels.

Recipe books for new Blenders and Mixers contain information on speed settings for other models in front, Instruction Section.

61

CRISP-FRIED FISH
6 servings

2 pounds fish fillets
1 cup buttermilk
Salt, pepper
1 cup packaged biscuit mix
Shortening

Soak fillets in buttermilk 30 minutes. Drain, sprinkle with salt and pepper. Dip fish in packaged biscuit mix. Fry in preheated shortening at 375° in Sunbeam Cooker and Deep Fryer until brown and tender. Drain on paper towels.

SHRIMP MOUSSE ELEGANTE
4 to 6 servings

2 egg whites
2 cups heavy cream
1 teaspoon salt
½ teaspoon white pepper
¼ teaspoon nutmeg
1 pound shrimp (raw), shelled
and cleaned
Sauce Elégante

Butter a 1-quart mold. Combine egg whites, cream and seasonings. Pour ⅓ of this mixture into Sunbeam Blender and add ⅓ of shrimp. Cover and process at Cream to a smooth paste. Empty into prepared mold. Repeat until all ingredients are used. Cover mold with aluminum foil. Place in pan with 1 inch water and bake 45 minutes in a preheated 350° F. oven. Let stand in mold 5 minutes. Turn out on warm platter and cover with Sauce Elégante.

SAUCE ELEGANTE
2¼ cups

1 can (10½ ounces) condensed
cream of mushroom soup
⅓ cup dry white wine
1 tablespoon butter
½ teaspoon tarragon (optional)
Dash black pepper
2 sprigs parsley
¼ pound cooked shrimp,
cleaned

Combine ingredients in Sunbeam Blender. Cover and process at Grate only until shrimp are chopped. Pour into saucepan. Heat slowly until hot. Pour over Shrimp Mousse.

FISH BALLS
6 to 8 servings

2 cups cooked or canned fish
2 cups cooked rice
2 eggs, beaten
½ teaspoon salt
⅛ teaspoon paprika
1 tablespoon lemon juice
1 teaspoon grated onion
2 tablespoons chopped parsley
Finely crushed cornflakes or
packaged cornflake crumbs

Flake cooked or canned fish, removing bones (drain liquid from canned fish). Combine fish, rice, eggs, salt, paprika, lemon juice, onion and parsley. Stir with a fork until well blended. Press into medium-sized balls. Roll in cornflake crumbs, coating well and patting into shape. Fry in preheated shortening at 375° in Sunbeam Cooker and Deep Fryer until browned, about 3 minutes. Drain. Put on paper towels. Serve with chili or tartar sauce.

MARINATED FISH
6 servings

¼ cup chopped onion
¼ cup ketchup
1 tablespoon vinegar
1 teaspoon Worcestershire sauce
3 tablespoons lemon juice
⅓ cup tomato juice
½ teaspoon celery salt
⅛ teaspoon pepper
2 pounds fish fillets
Fine dry bread crumbs

Combine onion, ketchup, vinegar, Worcestershire, lemon juice, tomato juice and seasonings. Cook mixture about 5 minutes. Cool, pour over fish and marinate several hours, covered, in refrigerator. Remove fish from mixture, drain and dip into bread crumbs. Fry in preheated shortening at 375° in Sunbeam Cooker and Deep Fryer until

brown and tender, about 5 minutes. Drain on paper towels.

BARBECUED FISH FILLETS
4 servings

5 tablespoons butter or
margarine, divided
½ cup diced onion
1 pound fish fillets
Salt, pepper
½ cup ketchup
⅓ cup lemon juice
2 teaspoons sugar
2 teaspoons Worcestershire
sauce
2 teaspoons prepared mustard

Preheat Multi-Cooker Frypan to 300°, add 2 tablespoons butter. When melted, add onions and sauté until golden. Remove. Add remaining butter. Cut fish fillets into serving portions. Brown lightly at 360°, turning carefully with a pancake turner. Spread onions over fish. Season with salt and pepper. Combine remaining ingredients and ¼ cup water; pour over fish. Simmer at 220° about 20 minutes until fish can be flaked easily.

BREADED FISH
PARMESAN
6 servings

½ cup grated Parmesan cheese
1 cup fine dry bread crumbs
¾ cup flour

Recipe books for new Blenders and Mixers
contain information on speed settings for
other models in front. Instruction Section.

63

2 teaspoons salt
¼ teaspoon pepper
½ teaspoon celery salt
1 egg
¼ cup milk or water
2 pounds fish fillets, steaks,
    or small fish
Shortening
¼ cup lemon juice
¼ cup finely chopped parsley
2 scallions, finely cut

Mix the Parmesan with the bread crumbs. Mix flour and seasonings. Beat egg slightly, stir in the milk or water. Cut fish into serving pieces. Dip first in seasoned flour, then in egg mixture, then in crumb-Parmesan mixture. Fry in preheated shortening at 375° in Sunbeam Cooker and Deep Fryer until golden brown and tender. Drain; place on paper towels. Combine remaining ingredients. Spoon this sauce over the fried fish served on a heated platter.

SCALLOPS CACCIATORE
4 servings

1 medium onion, quartered
1 medium green pepper,
    seeded and quartered
1 clove garlic
¼ cup cooking oil
1 pound scallops, cut into
    ¾-inch pieces
1 can (1 pound) tomatoes,
    drained
1 can (8 ounces) tomato sauce
¼ cup dry white wine

1¼ teaspoons salt
⅛ teaspoon pepper
2 bay leaves
2 tablespoons snipped parsley

Place onion, green pepper and garlic in Sunbeam Blender. Cover, set control at Chop. Use Touch-On switch two or three times. Heat oil in Multi-Cooker Frypan at 380°. Add scallops and cook about 5 minutes or until tender, turning as needed. Remove from Frypan. Add chopped mixture, turn heat to low and cook about 3 minutes or until tender. Add scallops, tomatoes, tomato sauce, wine, salt, pepper and bay leaves. Simmer gently about 5 minutes. Remove bay leaves. Serve hot, sprinkle with snipped parsley.

CODFISH CAKES
6 servings

1 pound salt codfish, shredded
4 cups raw potato, peeled and
    diced
2 tablespoons melted butter
    or margarine
⅛ teaspoon pepper
2 eggs, beaten
Flour
Shortening

Cover fish with cold water. Bring to a boil. Drain. Put potatoes and fish in saucepan with 2 cups cold water. Bring to a boil. Cook until potatoes are tender. Drain.

64

Mash with Mixmaster Mixer at No. 1. Add butter, pepper and eggs; beat at No. 8 until fluffy. Cool. Drop by tablespoonfuls into flour. Fry in preheated shortening at 400° in Sunbeam Cooker and Deep Fryer until browned, about 3 minutes. Lift basket to drain position. Drain. Then put on paper towels. Serve hot with chili sauce or tomato sauce.

SHRIMP BUFFET CASSEROLE
4 to 6 servings

2 tablespoons butter or
margarine
½ cup diced celery
2 scallions with tops, finely cut
1 can (10½ ounces) frozen
cream of shrimp soup
1⅓ cups milk
¼ green pepper, shredded
2 cups cooked and cleaned
shrimp (about 1 pound)
Dash pepper
½ cup sliced stuffed olives
½ cup grated cheese
Paprika

Melt butter in Multi-Cooker Frypan with Dial set at 260°. Add celery and scallions; sauté, stirring. Add frozen soup and milk. Turn Dial to Simmer; cover, opening to stir several times until soup is defrosted. Add green pepper, shrimp (cut in half if large), pepper and olives. Stir to blend. Cover, close vent; simmer 10 minutes. Sprinkle cheese

and paprika on top; cover, turn to Warm until ready to serve.

DEVILED SALMON
4 to 6 servings

1 can (1 pound) salmon, flaked
1 cup condensed tomato soup,
undiluted
¼ small onion
¼ small green pepper
3 tablespoons melted butter
½ teaspoon salt
1 teaspoon prepared mustard
1 slice lemon with peel

Preheat oven to 350° F. Put salmon in a buttered casserole. Put remaining ingredients into Sunbeam Blender. Cover and process at Chop until pepper and onion are chopped. Pour over salmon and bake 35 minutes.

ALMOND TOMATO FILLETS
4 servings

5 tablespoons butter or
margarine, divided
½ clove garlic, minced
4 cups chopped, peeled tomatoes
1 teaspoon salt, divided
½ teaspoon tarragon
¼ teaspoon pepper, divided
¼ cup flour
1 pound sole or flounder fillets
¼ cup blanched almonds,
slivered and toasted

Recipe books for new Blenders and Mixers
contain information on speed settings for
other models in front, Instruction Section.

65

In a saucepan heat 1 tablespoon of the butter. Add garlic and cook over medium heat, about 30 seconds. Add tomatoes, ½ teaspoon salt, tarragon and ⅛ teaspoon pepper. Cover and simmer over low heat while preparing fish. Combine flour, remaining salt and pepper. Coat fillets with flour mixture. Melt 4 tablespoons butter in Multi-Cooker Frypan at 380°. Add fillets and fry until golden brown on one side, 2 to 3 minutes; turn and brown other side until fish flakes easily when tested with a fork. Arrange tomato mixture on a shallow, heated serving platter. Place fillets on top. Sprinkle with almonds and serve immediately.

SEAFOOD MEDITERRANEE
4 to 6 servings

½ cup olive oil
3 cloves garlic, minced
6 small rock lobster-tails, cut into thirds
1 teaspoon oregano
1½ teaspoons salt
½ teaspoon pepper
1 can (1 pound) Italian plum tomatoes
1 cup dry white wine
2 bay leaves
1½ dozen cherrystone clams, scrubbed
1 pound shrimp, shelled and deveined
1 cup snipped parsley

Preheat Sunbeam Cooker and Deep Fryer to 300°. Add oil, garlic and cook, stirring, 1 minute. Add lobster pieces and cook, stirring, 3 minutes. Add oregano, salt, pepper, tomatoes, wine and bay leaves. Bring to a boil. Cover, lower heat to Simmer and cook 5 minutes. Add clams, shrimp and parsley. Bring mixture to a boil. Reduce heat to Simmer, cover and cook 5 minutes or until shrimp are cooked and the clams are open. Serve in soup bowls with French bread.

FRIED SHRIMP
6 servings

2 eggs
½ cup milk
1 cup sifted flour
1 teaspoon baking powder
1 teaspoon salt
2 teaspoons cooking oil
2 pounds shrimp
Shortening or oil

Put eggs into small bowl of Mixmaster Mixer and beat at No. 7 speed 1 minute. Turn Dial to No. 2. Add milk. Sift together flour, baking powder, salt. Add to milk and egg mixture. Add oil. Beat at No. 2 speed until smooth and well blended. Set aside. Remove shells of shrimp, leaving tail on. Cut partway through outside curve almost to either end. Lift out vein and flatten shrimp so that they stay open. Heat shortening in Sunbeam Cooker

Recipe books for new Blenders and Mixers contain information on speed settings for other models in front, Instruction Section.

and Deep Fryer at 375°. Dip shrimp one at a time into batter and cook a few at a time in the hot fat, about 4 minutes or until golden brown and puffy. Drain. Turn out on paper towels. Serve immediately with tartar sauce or cocktail sauce.

SCAMPI
4 servings

⅓ cup cooking oil
1 pound shrimp, shelled and deveined
2 tablespoons chopped celery
½ tablespoon chopped green pepper
1 tablespoon chopped onion
1 clove garlic, minced
1 tablespoon snipped parsley
2 tablespoons lemon juice
⅓ cup tomato paste
½ teaspoon salt

Heat oil in Multi-Cooker Frypan to 280°. Add shrimp, celery, green pepper, onion and garlic. Sauté, turning often until shrimp are just pink. Turn heat to Simmer. Add ⅓ cup water and remaining ingredients and mix well. Simmer, stirring occasionally, about 5 minutes or until shrimp are tender.

FISH DUGLERE
4 servings

4 fish fillets
1 teaspoon salt

Pepper, freshly ground
5 tablespoons butter or margarine, divided
1 medium onion, chopped
1 clove garlic
4 ripe tomatoes, peeled and chopped
1 tablespoon snipped parsley
¼ cup dry white wine
1 tablespoon flour

Season fish fillets with salt and pepper. Melt 3 tablespoons of the butter in Multi-Cooker Frypan at 280°. Add onion and garlic and cook gently until onion is soft. Place fish fillets in pan. Arrange tomatoes and parsley over fish. Add wine and ½ cup water. Cover tightly and simmer at 240° about 8 minutes or until fish flakes easily when tested with a fork. Remove fish to a hot platter. Turn up heat and boil liquid until it is reduced to ⅓ its original quantity. Remove garlic. Cream together flour and remaining 2 tablespoons butter. Stir into mixture in Frypan and cook, stirring until mixture comes to a boil and is thickened. Pour sauce over hot fish.

SOLE
IN MOUSSELINE SAUCE
6 servings

6 fillets of sole
Salt, pepper
½ cup dry white wine
3 egg yolks

Dash cayenne pepper
½ cup butter
¼ cup heavy cream

Wipe fillets with paper towels. Sprinkle with salt and pepper and roll up each fillet. Secure with toothpicks. Heat wine in Multi-Cooker Frypan with a dash of salt at 280°. Add sole, cover and simmer about 5 minutes or until opaque. Remove sole and place in a baking dish. Boil down wine to 2 tablespoonfuls. Place in Sunbeam Blender. Add egg yolks, a pinch of salt and cayenne. Cover and process at Cream for a few seconds. Heat butter until it is foaming hot. Remove Feeder Cap and pour butter in a steady stream until mixture is thickened. Turn sauce out of Blender into a bowl and cool slightly. Whip cream in Blender or with a Mixmaster Hand Mixer at highest setting until stiff. Fold cream into sauce. Spoon over poached fillets. Bake 10 minutes in a preheated 400° F. oven or until fish flakes easily when tested with a fork.

LOBSTER CANTONESE
4 servings

3 tablespoons cooking oil
1 clove garlic, crushed
½ pound coarsely ground lean
    pork
¼ cup soy sauce

2 cups chicken broth
1 teaspoon sugar
2 1-pound lobsters, cut into
    2-inch pieces
2 tablespoons cornstarch
1 bunch scallions, cut into
½-inch chunks, including
    some green top
1 egg, slightly beaten

Preheat Multi-Cooker Frypan to 340°. Heat oil. Add garlic and pork and sauté until the pork loses its pink color. Stir in soy sauce, chicken broth and sugar and bring to a boil. Add lobster. Cover, reduce heat to Simmer and cook 10 minutes. Combine cornstarch and ¼ cup cold water in a small bowl to a smooth paste. Add to the lobster and stir until sauce is thickened and clear. Stir in scallions. Pour the slightly beaten egg over the lobster and cook, stirring just until the egg is set. Serve immediately.

SOLE BELLE AURORE
6 servings

6 sole or flounder fillets
3 tablespoons butter
1 tablespoon minced onion
½ cup clam juice
Pinch salt
Pepper, freshly ground
½ cup non-dairy powdered
    cream
3 tablespoons flour
¼ cup minced parsley

Halve the fillets lengthwise; roll and tie with thread or secure

Recipe books for new Blenders and Mixers
contain information on speed settings for
other models in front, Instruction Section.

69

with toothpicks. Melt butter in Multi-Cooker Frypan at 340°. Add onion and cook until just very lightly browned. Add fillets and cook until lightly browned. Add clam juice, salt and pepper. Bring just to a boil. Turn Frypan Dial to Simmer; cover and cook 8 to 10 minutes or until fillets flake easily when tested with a fork. Remove fish to a shallow oven-proof casserole. Combine powdered cream and flour. Blend into hot liquid in Frypan. Stir in 1 cup boiling water. Cook at 280°, stirring constantly until mixture thickens. Stir in parsley and pour sauce over fish in casserole. Preheat broiler or Broiler Cover Frypan. Place casserole under broiler and brown lightly.

CHINESE SUPPER
4 servings

½ pound raw medium shrimp,
    shelled
2 tablespoons salad oil
½ pound ground lean pork
⅓ cup finely chopped scallions,
    with some of green tops
2 cups thinly sliced mushrooms
1 cup chicken stock
1 tablespoon soy sauce
1 package (7 ounces) frozen
    snow peas
(edible pea pods), partially
    thawed

Preheat Multi-Cooker Frypan to 325°. Cut the shrimp into lengthwise halves. Rinse well. In the oil, stir-fry the pork until lightly browned. Add shrimp halves and scallions and stir-fry 2 minutes. Stir in mushrooms. Blend chicken stock and soy sauce and stir into Frypan. Simmer at 250° 2 minutes. Add snow peas, mix gently. Turn heat up to 425°. Cook 2 to 3 minutes or until snow peas are thawed and cooked, but still crisp. Serve immediately.

Serving style: Serve with fluffy white rice.

SEASIDE LOAF
6 servings

¼ cup lemon juice
1 tablespoon gelatin
1¼ cups hot water
3 tablespoons sugar
½ teaspoon salt
¼ cup cider vinegar
¾ cup diced celery
¼ cup sliced sweet pickles
1 medium avocado, peeled,
    seeded, sliced
1 cup flaked tuna fish

Put lemon juice and gelatin into Sunbeam Blender; add water, sugar, salt and vinegar. Process at Stir until gelatin is dissolved. Add celery, pickles and avocado; blender-chop vegetables. Stir in tuna. Pour into oiled loaf pan. Chill until firm. Slice and serve with mayonnaise.

VARIETY IN VEGETABLES AND SIDE DISHES

There's more to serving vegetables than boiling and buttering them, more to starches than a choice between rice and potatoes. Here you'll find adventurous new approaches to the vegetable-and-side-dish problem, all of them fun to make, fun to eat. Some can be cooked at the table, and many served, hot and appetizing, directly from your Sunbeam Appliances.

GOLDEN ONIONS
4 to 6 servings

3 tablespoons butter or
margarine
3 Spanish onions, sliced
1 tablespoon curry powder
(more or less)

Heat Multi-Cooker Frypan to 320°. Melt butter, add onions. Cook, turning often and breaking into rings until tender and pale golden. Sprinkle with curry powder to taste before serving.

CORN PUDDING
6 servings

3 eggs
3 tablespoons melted butter
or margarine
1 tablespoon sugar
1 tablespoon flour
1½ teaspoons salt
1⅓ cups milk, scalded
¼-inch slice small onion
1½ cups whole kernel corn

Butter a 2-quart casserole. Put eggs into Sunbeam Blender; cover, process at Stir until beaten. Add remaining ingredients; cover, process at Whip only until corn is thoroughly mixed into batter. Pour into casserole. Bake 1 hour 10 minutes in preheated 350° F. oven.

POTATO PUFFS
4 to 6 servings

2 cups cold mashed potatoes
1 egg, beaten
½ teaspoon salt
⅛ teaspoon pepper
½ cup grated American cheese
Fine dry crumbs
Shortening

Combine potatoes, egg, salt, pepper and cheese. Shape into balls and roll in crumbs. Preheat Sunbeam Cooker and Deep Fryer to 375°. Fry balls in heated shortening until brown, about 3 minutes. Lift basket to drain supports. Drain. Put puffs on paper towels. Serve hot.

Recipe books for new Blenders and Mixers
contain information on speed settings for
other models in front, Instruction Section.

71

FRENCH FRIED ONIONS

Large onions, sliced crosswise
¼ inch thick
Seasoned flour
1 egg
¼ cup milk
Fine dry crumbs
Fat for deep frying
Salt

Separate onion slices into rings and dip into seasoned flour, then into the egg beaten with the milk. Dip into crumbs and shake to remove excess. Fry in pre-heated shortening at 375° in Sunbeam Cooker and Deep Fryer until browned, about 3 minutes. Drain and place on paper towels. Sprinkle with salt; serve hot.

PENNSYLVANIA RED CABBAGE
6 servings

1 medium head red cabbage
½ teaspoon caraway seeds
½ cup vinegar
½ cup brown sugar
1½ teaspoons salt
Dash pepper
2 medium apples, cored and cut
in quarters
2 tablespoons salad oil or bacon
drippings

Blender-chop cabbage. Empty into a saucepan and add caraway seeds. Put ½ cup water and the remaining ingredients into Blender. Cover and process at Chop until apples are coarsely chopped. Pour over cabbage. Cover and simmer 1 hour.

SAUTEED MUSHROOMS
4 servings

¼ cup butter or margarine
1 tablespoon grated onion
(optional)
1 pound fresh mushrooms,
sliced
Salt, pepper
Lemon juice

Preheat Multi-Cooker Frypan to 340°. Add butter and melt. Add the onion and sauté a few minutes; then add mushrooms. Sauté, stirring frequently, about 5 to 8 minutes. Sprinkle with salt, pepper and lemon juice.

Good to know: Canned mushrooms may be drained and sautéed in the same manner.

Another way: Omit the lemon juice and add 2 tablespoons of sherry and 5 tablespoons of cream.

CANDIED SWEET POTATOES
6 servings

¼ cup butter or margarine
1 cup brown sugar, firmly packed
¼ cup orange juice

½ teaspoon salt
1 teaspoon grated orange rind
6 medium sweet potatoes, peeled,
cut in half lengthwise, cooked
Chopped nuts (optional)

Preheat Multi-Cooker Frypan to 320°. Combine butter, brown sugar, juice, salt and rind or cinnamon in Frypan. Boil, stirring, about 2 minutes. Add sweet potatoes to syrup and simmer 10 minutes at about 220°, spooning syrup over potatoes frequently and turning. Serve hot; garnish with chopped nuts, if desired.

FRENCH FRIED
POTATOES
(Blanch and brown method)

Mature white potatoes, peeled
3 pounds shortening
Salt

Cut potatoes into ⅜-inch slices, then into lengthwise strips ⅜ inch wide. Wash in cold water. Dry well between towels. Meanwhile, preheat shortening to 375° in Sunbeam Cooker and Deep Fryer. Fill the basket not more than ⅓ full. Lower slowly into preheated shortening and fry until potatoes are tender but not brown, about 5 to 7 minutes. Lift basket to drain supports. Drain. Then put potatoes on double-thick paper towels on a baking sheet. Repeat until all potatoes are partially fried, preheating Deep Fryer to 375° be-

fore each batch. Cover with wax paper and set aside. Just before serving, preheat the shortening in Deep Fryer to 400°. Fill basket half full. Lower into shortening. Finish frying until browned and crisp, about 3 to 5 minutes, shaking basket occasionally to turn potatoes. Lift basket to drain supports. Drain. Place potatoes on paper towels. Sprinkle with salt. Serve at once. (Frying time varies with kind and maturity of potatoes.)

FRENCH FRIED
POTATOES
(Start to finish—one frying)

Mature white potatoes
3 pounds shortening
Salt

Pare potatoes, cut into ⅜-inch strips. Wash in cold water, dry well between towels. Meanwhile preheat shortening to 375° in Sunbeam Cooker and Deep Fryer. Fill basket about ⅓ full. Slowly lower potatoes into hot shortening. Fry until browned and crisp, about 10 to 15 minutes. Shake basket occasionally to turn potatoes. Lift basket to drain supports. Drain. Put potatoes on paper towels. Sprinkle with salt. Serve at once.
Good to know: Potatoes may also be cut into balls, julienne, cubes or lattice.
For potato chips: cut peeled potatoes into very thin slices on a

Recipe books for new Blenders and Mixers
contain information on speed settings for
other models in front, Instruction Section.

vegetable cutter. Soak in ice water about one hour, then drain and dry on towels. Fry in preheated shortening at 375° in Sunbeam Cooker and Deep Fryer until brown, about 5 minutes. Shake basket frequently to keep potatoes from sticking together. Drain. Put on paper towels. Sprinkle with salt.

SAUTEED ONIONS
4 servings

4 onions, sliced ¼ inch thick
3 tablespoons butter or
margarine

Preheat Multi-Cooker Frypan to 300°. Add butter and melt. Add onions and sauté, stirring frequently until golden in color. Sprinkle with salt. Serve over chops, hamburgers, steak or liver, etc.

CHEESE POTATO PATTIES
4 servings

3 tablespoons butter
2 teaspoons instant minced
onion
2 cups cold, leftover mashed
potatoes
¾ cup grated American cheese
1 teaspoon dried dillweed
1 teaspoon salt

Preheat Multi-Cooker Frypan to 320°. Melt 2 tablespoons of the butter. Add onion and sauté

until golden brown. Remove onion to a bowl. Combine with remaining ingredients. Blend well. Divide mixture into 4 portions and shape into patties. Put remaining tablespoon butter in Frypan. Fry patties until golden brown on both sides.

MASHED POTATOES
4 to 6 servings

6 medium potatoes
⅓ to ⅔ cup hot milk or
part cream
2 to 3 tablespoons butter or
margarine
1 teaspoon salt
Dash pepper, if desired

Pare potatoes and cook in boiling salted water until tender. Drain. Place over low heat for a few minutes to dry out, shaking frequently. When mealy, turn into large Mixmaster Mixer bowl. Beat at No. 1 speed, lifting beaters slightly, to chop potatoes, about 1 minute. Combine hot milk, butter, salt and pepper. Pour over potatoes, whip at No. 8 speed about 2 minutes, adding enough milk to make fluffy. Serve at once.

STUFFED TOMATOES
6 servings

6 slices bread
6 firm tomatoes
1 small onion
6 sprigs parsley

Recipe books for new Blenders and Mixers contain information on speed settings for other models in front, Instruction Section.

2 egg yolks
½ teaspoon salt
¼ teaspoon pepper
2 tablespoons butter

Butter a baking dish. Blender-crumb bread. Wash and dry tomatoes, cut off tops and remove pulp. Sprinkle insides of shells with salt and pepper. Put tomato pulp, onion, parsley, egg yolks and seasonings into Sunbeam Blender; cover and process at Chop until parsley and onion are finely chopped. Mix with bread crumbs. Melt butter in saucepan, add tomato mixture and cook over low heat about 10 minutes. Fill tomatoes with this mixture. Sprinkle bread crumbs on top, if desired. Bake 20 to 25 minutes in a preheated 350° F. oven until soft.

INDIAN SUMMER VEGETABLES
10 to 12 servings

2 ears fresh corn
3 tablespoons butter or margarine
2 medium-sized green peppers, cut into strips
2 medium onions, sliced
6 medium zucchini, cut into ½-inch slices
4 medium tomatoes, quartered
1½ teaspoons salt
¼ teaspoon coarsely ground black pepper

¼ teaspoon sweet basil
½ cup grated Parmesan cheese

Cut corn off the cob. Preheat Multi-Cooker Frypan to 360°. Add butter and melt. Add green peppers and onions. Cover and cook 5 minutes, stir once or twice. Add ¼ cup water and remaining ingredients except Parmesan. Cover and cook 10 minutes or until vegetables are crisply tender, not mushy. Shake occasionally during cooking time. Serve sprinkled with grated cheese.

ORIENTAL-STYLE BROCCOLI
5 to 6 servings

½ pound flank steak
1½ pounds broccoli
2 teaspoons sherry
⅛ teaspoon pepper
2 teaspoons soy sauce
½ teaspoon salt
½ teaspoon sugar
¼ cup salad oil
2 teaspoons cornstarch

Put meat in freezer about 15 minutes before starting preparation. Cut cold meat into thin slices, across grain of meat and at a slant, using Sunbeam Knife. Wash broccoli; cut flowerets from stalk. Cut stalks into diagonal ¼-inch slices. Combine sherry, pepper, soy sauce, salt, sugar and ½ cup water. Preheat Multi-Cooker Frypan to 360°. Heat 2 tablespoons of the

Recipe books for new Blenders and Mixers contain information on speed settings for other models in front, Instruction Section.

oil; add broccoli-stalk slices. Cover Frypan; shake a little and cook 2 minutes. Add broccoli flowerets; cover and cook another 2 minutes. Broccoli should now be crisply tender. Remove broccoli to a warm plate. Put remaining oil in hot skillet. Add sliced meat. Brown quickly on both sides. Pour in soy sauce mixture. Cover and cook 2 minutes. Add cooked broccoli. Dissolve cornstarch in ¼ cup water. Add to broccoli mixture. Stir and bring to a boil. Serve immediately.

SPECIAL CARROTS
6 servings

5 large carrots, grated
2 eggs
2 tablespoons flour
½ teaspoon salt
¼ teaspoon white pepper
¼ cup chopped pecans
3 tablespoons cooking oil, divided
2 onions, thinly sliced
2 stalks celery, diced
1 green pepper, seeded, in chunks
1½ cups peeled, seeded, chopped tomatoes
¼ cup tomato paste
¼ cup brown sugar

Combine carrots, eggs, flour, salt, pepper and pecans. Preheat Multi-Cooker Frypan to 350°. Place 2 tablespoons of the oil in Frypan. Drop mixture into Frypan by teaspoonfuls. Fry until

these patties are brown on both sides. Drain on paper towels. Add remaining oil to Frypan; add remaining ingredients. Turn Frypan temperature to Simmer and cook vegetables 10 minutes, stirring occasionally. Taste and season. Carefully add patties; simmer, covered, 10 minutes.

FRIED CHEESE
4 to 6 servings

1-pound Mozzarella cheese
½ cup flour
2 eggs, slightly beaten
½ cup fine dry bread crumbs
2 tablespoons butter or margarine

Cut Mozzarella into ¼-inch slices. Preheat Multi-Cooker Frypan to 400°. Dip each slice of cheese into flour, then into beaten egg, then into bread crumbs. Melt butter in Frypan. Sauté Mozzarella slices about 2 minutes on each side (turn with a pancake turner) or until nicely browned.

SKILLET ZUCCHINI
4 to 6 servings

¼ cup butter or margarine
6 small zucchini, cut into ¼-inch slices
1 onion, thinly sliced
1 teaspoon salt
Dash pepper
2 tomatoes, cut into chunks

¼ cup shredded Cheddar cheese
1 tablespoon soy sauce

Heat Multi-Cooker Frypan to 300°. Melt butter; add zucchini, onion, seasonings, tomatoes and ¼ cup water. Cover and cook 10 minutes. Sprinkle with Cheddar and soy sauce; cover and cook 2 minutes.

BAKED CARROT PUFFS
6 to 8 servings

2 pounds carrots, pared and sliced
1 teaspoon salt
Graham crackers
6 tablespoons butter or margarine, divided
Dash ground ginger
2 eggs, separated
¼ cup light brown sugar
¼ cup fine dry bread crumbs

Preheat oven to 375° F. Cook carrots with ½ cup water and salt, about 15 minutes or until tender. Break a few graham crackers into Sunbeam Blender. Cover and process at Crumb. Empty crumbs into a measuring cup. Continue until there is ¾ cup graham cracker crumbs. Empty into large bowl of Mixmaster Mixer. Drain liquid from cooked carrots. Place carrots in Blender. Cover and process at Puree until smooth. Turn into large bowl of Mixer. Add 4 tablespoons of the butter, ginger and egg yolks. Beat at No. 4 until smooth. Cool. Beat egg whites in small bowl of Mixmaster Mixer at No. 12 speed until they form firm peaks. Fold into carrot mixture. Turn mixture into a 3-quart casserole. Combine remaining 2 tablespoons butter with brown sugar and bread crumbs. Sprinkle over top. Bake 40 minutes.

POTATO PANCAKES
6 servings

2 eggs
½ small onion
1 teaspoon salt
2 tablespoons flour
¼ teaspoon baking powder
3 cups cubed raw potatoes

Put eggs, onion, salt, flour, baking powder and ½ cup potato cubes into Sunbeam Blender. Cover and process at Grate until potatoes are grated. Add remaining potatoes, cover and process at Chop only until potato cubes have been processed. Do not overblend. Use a rubber spatula to guide potatoes to blades. Preheat Sunbeam Griddle to 380°. Grease Griddle lightly. Pour mixture onto hot Griddle in desired size. Fry until golden brown on both sides. Drain on paper towels.

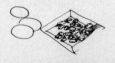

A BOUNTY OF BEVERAGES

Delicious meal accompaniments, tasty between-meal and after-school snacks, wonderful additions to the menu on any occasion when you are entertaining, even whole-meal wonders—here are beverages that the entire family· will enjoy. With your Sunbeam Blender as your helper, whip up these many kinds of delectable drinks in practically no time at all.

STRAWBERRY SMOOTHEE
2 cups

1 cup cold milk
¾ cup strawberries
1 tablespoon sugar
1 teaspoon lemon juice
1 cup crushed ice
Grated nutmeg

Put all ingredients except nutmeg into Sunbeam Blender; cover and process at Drinks until smooth. Top with grated nutmeg.

APRI-COFFEE FROST
1 quart

1 cup chilled apricot nectar
1⅓ cups cold strong coffee
½ pint coffee ice cream, softened
⅔ cup milk
½ teaspoon almond extract

Combine all ingredients in Sunbeam Blender. Cover and process at Stir until smooth. Serve in tall chilled glasses.

MEXICAN CHOCOLATE
2½ cups

½ cup semisweet chocolate chips
1 tablespoon instant coffee powder
½ teaspoon vanilla extract
¼ teaspoon cinnamon
2 cups hot milk

Put all ingredients into Sunbeam Blender; cover and process at Drinks until chips are dissolved. Serve hot.

COLD EGGNOG
1 quart

3 cups cold milk
3 eggs

Recipe books for new Blenders and Mixers
contain information on speed settings for
other models in front, Instruction Section.

79

3 tablespoons sugar
½ teaspoon vanilla extract
¼ teaspoon salt
1 cup crushed ice

Put all ingredients into Sunbeam Blender; cover and process at Drinks until smooth.

LEMON-STRAWBERRY PUNCH
32 servings

1½ cups strawberries
½ cup sugar
3 cans (6 ounces each) frozen
lemonade concentrate
1 quart chilled ginger ale

Wash and hull berries. Place in Sunbeam Blender. Add sugar and lemonade concentrate. Add 3 lemonade cans water. Cover and process at Drinks until smooth. Pour mixture into a punch bowl. Add ginger ale and mix well. Add block of ice. Serve chilled.

HOT CHOCOLATE
2½ cups

2 squares unsweetened
chocolate, cut into pieces
⅓ cup sugar
¼ teaspoon vanilla extract
2 cups hot milk
¼ teaspoon salt

Put all ingredients into Sunbeam Blender; cover and process at Stir until chocolate is dissolved.

SPICY APPLE EGGNOG
1 quart

2 eggs, separated
½ cup heavy cream, whipped
¼ cup sugar
½ teaspoon salt
½ teaspoon cinnamon
Dash nutmeg
⅔ cup apple juice
3 cups scalded milk

Beat egg whites with Mixmaster Hand Mixer at highest speed until stiff. Blender-whip cream and set aside. Put egg yolks, sugar, salt, cinnamon, nutmeg and apple juice into Sunbeam Blender; cover and process at Stir until sugar is dissolved. Remove Feeder Cap and add scalded milk slowly. When well blended, pour over egg whites and quickly fold together. Serve hot, topped with a mound of whipped cream.

BREAKFAST IN A GLASS
1 serving, 250 calories

1 cup skim milk
1 egg
½ cup fresh fruit

Put all ingredients into Sunbeam Blender; cover and process at Drinks until well blended. Chill before serving.

liquefied. Divide evenly among four tall glasses. Fill with ginger ale; stir gently to mix. Serve with peppermint candy canes as stirrers.

SUNBEAM SLIMMER
1 quart

1 egg
2 tablespoons corn oil
1¼ cups skim milk powder
1 teaspoon vanilla extract
Artificial sweetener

Put all ingredients and 3 cups water into Sunbeam Blender. Cover and process at Drinks until well blended. Chill before serving. Divide into three servings for full day's menu of approximately 950 calories.

PEACH COOLER
1½ cups

¾ cup cold milk
½ cup chilled cut-up peaches,
fresh or canned
¼ teaspoon salt
2 or 3 drops almond extract
½ cup vanilla ice cream, in
6 pieces (serving consistency)

Put all ingredients except ice cream into Sunbeam Blender; cover and process at Drinks until smooth. Stop and add the ice cream; cover and process at Stir 3 to 5 seconds.

CANDY CANE PUNCH
4 servings

½ cup lemon juice
1 can (6 ounces) frozen orange
juice concentrate
¼ cup sugar
1 egg white
6 hard peppermint candies
Ginger ale
4 peppermint candy canes

Put all ingredients except candy canes and ginger ale into Sunbeam Blender; cover and process at Liquefy until candies are

MINT MALT
4 servings

3 tablespoons crushed
peppermint-stick candy
1½ cups milk
¼ cup chocolate-flavored
malted milk powder
Dash salt
1 teaspoon vanilla
1 pint chocolate ice cream
Whipped cream

Combine half of the peppermint-stick candy, ½ cup milk, malted

Recipe books for new Blenders and Mixers
contain information on speed settings for
other models in front, Instruction Section.

81

milk powder, salt and vanilla in Sunbeam Blender. Cover and process at Liquefy until candy is dissolved. Add ice cream and remaining milk. Process at Stir until blended. Pour into 4 chilled glasses. Top with whipped cream. Sprinkle remaining candy on top. Serve with candy cane sticks for stirrers.

CARROT-PINEAPPLE COCKTAIL
3 cups

2 cups pineapple juice
2 medium carrots, cut in 1-inch pieces
1 slice lemon, ¼ inch thick
1 cup crushed ice

Put juice, carrots and lemon into Sunbeam Blender; cover and process at Liquefy until carrots are liquefied. Remove cover and add ice. Continue processing until ice is liquefied.

PINEAPPLE MINT SPLASH
3 cups

1 cup cubed pineapple, fresh or canned
3 oranges, peeled and cut up

¼ cup after-dinner mints
1 cup crushed ice

Put ½ cup water and all ingredients except ice into Sunbeam Blender; cover and process at Liquefy until pineapple is liquefied. Remove cover and add ice; continue to process until ice is liquefied.

PINK LASSIES
2½ cups

1 cup cranberry juice
¼ cup orange juice
1 cup vanilla ice cream (serving consistency)

Put all ingredients into Sunbeam Blender; cover and process at Drinks until smooth. Serve in cocktail glasses with straws.

FRESHLY GROUND COFFEE

Freshly ground coffee is easily and quickly prepared in the Sunbeam Blender. It's best not to grind more than a day's supply at one time, since ground coffee loses flavor rapidly. Process at Grate.

Approximate timing:

Percolator	20 to 30 seconds
Drip	35 to 40 seconds
Very fine drip	50 to 60 seconds

Recipe books for new Blenders and Mixers contain information on speed settings for other models in front, Instruction Section.

TOMATO JUICE COCKTAIL
3½ cups

2 cups tomato juice
1 thin slice lemon with peel
2 sprigs parsley
½-inch strip green pepper
8-inch rib celery, cut in
1-inch pieces
½-inch slice cucumber,
unpeeled
¼ teaspoon Worcestershire
sauce
½ teaspoon salt
1 cup crushed ice

Put all ingredients except ice into Sunbeam Blender; cover and process at Liquefy until all ingredients are liquefied. Remove cover and add ice; continue to process until the ice is liquefied.

CHOCOLATE MILK
SHAKE, MALTED
1 drink

¾ cup cold milk
2 tablespoons chocolate syrup
Malted milk powder (optional)
½ to 1 cup vanilla ice cream
(serving consistency)

Put milk and syrup (and malted milk powder if desired) into Sunbeam Blender; cover and process at Stir until thoroughly blended. Stop and add the ice cream, spooning it into the Blender in about 8 pieces. Cover and process at Drinks only 3 to 5 seconds. (Longer processing will liquefy the ice cream.)

DAIQUIRI
2 drinks

3 ounces light rum
2 tablespoons lime or lemon
juice
2 teaspoons powdered sugar
1½ cups crushed ice

Put all ingredients into Sunbeam Blender, cover and process at Drinks until well blended.

WHISKEY SOUR
2 drinks

4 ounces whiskey
2 tablespoons lemon juice
1 teaspoon sugar
1 cup crushed ice

Put all ingredients into Sunbeam Blender, cover and process at Drinks until well blended.

GRASSHOPPER
3 drinks

3 ounces white crème de cacao
3 ounces green crème de menthe
2 tablespoons heavy cream

or ½ cup ice cream
½ cup crushed ice

Put all ingredients into Sunbeam Blender, cover and process at Drinks until well blended.

SCARLETT O'HARA
1 drink

1 teaspoon lime juice
1½ ounces bourbon
1 ounce cranberry juice
½ cup crushed ice

Put all ingredients into Sunbeam Blender, cover and process at Drinks until well blended.

COFFEE COCKTAIL
1 drink

1 ounce brandy
1 ounce cointreau
1 ounce cold black coffee
½ cup crushed ice

Put all ingredients into Sunbeam Blender, cover and process at Drinks until well blended.

ALEXANDER
2 drinks

2 ounces gin
2 ounces crème de cacao

2 ounces heavy cream or
1 scoop ice cream
½ cup crushed ice

Put all ingredients into Sunbeam Blender, cover and process at Drinks until well blended.
Brandy Alexander: Substitute brandy for gin.

ORANGE BLOSSOM
2 drinks

3 ounces gin or light rum
3 ounces orange juice
2 teaspoons powdered sugar
1 cup crushed ice

Put all ingredients into Sunbeam Blender, cover and process at Drinks until well blended.

For a thicker, creamy drink: Substitute 2 scoops vanilla ice cream and 1 scoop orange sherbet for the orange juice, sugar and ice.

COLLINS
2 drinks

3 ounces gin or rum
3 ounces lime or lemon juice
2 tablespoons powdered sugar
1 cup crushed ice
Club soda

Put all ingredients except the Club soda into Sunbeam Blender, cover and process at

Recipe books for new Blenders and Mixers
contain information on speed settings for
other models in front, Instruction Section.

85

Drinks until well blended. Pour
over ice cubes, add club soda.

BLOODY MARY
2 drinks

6 ounces tomato juice
½ ounce lemon juice
4 ounces vodka
3 dashes Worcestershire sauce
Salt, pepper, red pepper to taste
1 cup crushed ice

Put all ingredients into Sunbeam
Blender, cover and process at
Drinks until well blended. Strain
if desired.

BACARDI COCKTAIL
6 drinks

*1 can (6 ounces) frozen pink
lemonade*
1 can (6 ounces) frozen limeade
2 cans (12 ounces) light rum
Dash grenadine

Put all ingredients into Sunbeam
Blender, cover and process at
Drinks until well blended.

SCREWDRIVER
2 drinks

1 cup orange juice
3 ounces vodka
1 cup crushed ice

Put all ingredients into Sunbeam
Blender, cover and process at
Drinks until well blended.

PINK LADY
2 drinks

3 ounces gin
1½ ounces apple brandy
2 tablespoons lemon juice
1 tablespoon grenadine
1 egg white
1 cup crushed ice

Put all ingredients into Sunbeam
Blender, cover and process at
Drinks until well blended.

EGGNOG
2 drinks

*6 ounces rum, brandy, whiskey,
sherry or Cognac*
1 egg
2 tablespoons powdered sugar
1¼ cups milk
½ cup crushed ice
Nutmeg

Put all ingredients into Sunbeam
Blender, cover and process at
Drinks until well blended. Strain
if desired; sprinkle with nutmeg.

SAVORY SALADS, DRESSINGS AND SAUCES

Whole-meal salads, side-dish salads, molded salads, even some hot ones—salads to add pleasure to meals the year around, plus a bonus of tasty dressings and a wonderful collection of sauces to add a finishing touch to many kinds of dishes. Let your Sunbeam Blender and Mixmaster Mixer be your "extra pairs of hands" in preparing these delightful—and easy—recipes.

BAKED CHICKEN SALAD
4 to 6 servings

1 cup potato chip crumbs
(about 4 cups whole chips)
2 cups diced cold chicken
1½ cups sliced celery
½ cup Blender Mayonnaise
(page 93)
1 cup cubed Cheddar cheese
1 slice lemon, seeded and peeled
½ small onion, cut in half
¼ cup almonds

Grease a 2-quart casserole. Crumb potato chips in Sunbeam Blender. Reserve. Put chicken and celery into casserole. Put mayonnaise, Cheddar, lemon and onion into Blender; cover and process at Cream until smooth. Remove Feeder Cap; add almonds, processing only until chopped. Pour over chicken and celery, and mix. Sprinkle potato chip crumbs over top. Bake in a preheated 375° F. oven 30 minutes.

MIDEASTERN CHICKEN SALAD
4 servings

1¼ cups chicken consommé
1 cup walnuts
4 blanched almonds
1 teaspoon minced onion
¼ cup soft bread crumbs
½ teaspoon salt
½ teaspoon paprika
Boston lettuce
3 cups cubed cold cooked
chicken
Capers

Place first 7 ingredients in Sunbeam Blender. Cover and process at Cream 1 minute. Place leaves of Boston lettuce on 4 serving plates and divide chicken over them. Spoon sauce over chicken. Sprinkle with capers.

Serving style: Serve this frankly elegant chicken salad with cold asparagus vinaigrette and hot buttered rolls to make a luncheon your guests will remember.

Recipe books for new Blenders and Mixers contain information on speed settings for other models in front, Instruction Section.

87

PEACH-ALMOND
SOUFFLE SALAD
4 to 6 servings

1 package (3 ounces) orange-
flavored gelatin
2 tablespoons lemon juice
½ cup mayonnaise
¼ teaspoon salt
1½ cup diced cling peaches,
well drained
1 package (3 ounces) cream
cheese, softened
¼ cup toasted slivered almonds

Pour 1 cup hot water over gelatin in large bowl of Mixmaster Mixer. Stir until gelatin is dissolved. Add ½ cup cold water, lemon juice, mayonnaise and salt. Beat at No. 5 until well mixed. Pour into freezing tray. Chill in freezer or refrigerator until firm, about 20 to 25 minutes. Meanwhile combine peaches, cheese and almonds. Turn gelatin mixture back into chilled mixer bowl. Beat at No. 10 speed until fluffy and thick. Fold in peach mixture. Pour into a 1-quart mold. Chill until firm. Unmold on chilled serving plate and garnish as desired.

STRASSBURG SALAD
6 servings

½ cup nuts
3 cups cabbage cut into pieces
1 cup crushed pineapple,
drained
2 bananas, sliced
¼ cup mayonnaise
½ cup heavy cream

Place nuts in Sunbeam Blender. Cover and process at Chop; empty into a large bowl. Chop cabbage in same manner, add to nuts. Add pineapple and bananas to cabbage. Put mayonnaise and cream into Blender; cover and process at Whip until thick. Fold into cabbage mixture. Chill before serving.

HERBED CHICKEN AND
OLIVE MOUSSE
8 servings

2 envelopes unflavored gelatin
2½ cups hot chicken broth
⅛ teaspoon garlic powder
1 teaspoon onion powder
½ teaspoon ground thyme
1¼ teaspoons dry mustard
Dash cayenne pepper
2 tablespoons lemon juice
2 teaspoons salt
1 cup heavy cream
⅓ cup diced black olives
2½ cups diced cold chicken

Soften gelatin in ½ cup cold water in Sunbeam Blender. Add hot chicken broth. Cover and process at Stir until gelatin is dissolved. Add next 7 ingredients. Cover and process at Stir. Pour mixture into a bowl and chill in refrigerator until mixture begins to thicken. Rinse out Blender container and pour in cream. Cover and process at Whip until stiff. Fold olives and chicken into gelatin mixture. Fold in whipped cream. Turn mixture into a 1½-quart mold. Chill until firm. Unmold on a chilled serving platter. Garnish as desired.

SALAD OF GOLD
6 to 8 servings

1 package (3 ounces) lemon-
flavored gelatin
1 can (12 ounces) crushed
pineapple
2 tablespoons vinegar
⅔ cup evaporated milk
2 packages (3 ounces each)
cream cheese cut into 1-inch
pieces
1 cup carrot pieces

Oil a 1-quart ring mold. Put gelatin and ⅔ cup very hot water into Sunbeam Blender; cover and process at Stir until dissolved. Drain pineapple and measure ⅔ cup juice and ⅔ cup pineapple. Reserve pineapple. Remove Feeder Cap and add juice, vinegar and milk. Add cream cheese, one piece at a time; process at Beat. When cheese is blended, add carrot and pineapple, all at one time. Cover and process at Grate only

until carrots are grated. Pour into prepared mold. Chill until set.

CRANBERRY MOLD
6 servings

1 envelope unflavored gelatin
1 package (3 ounces) cherry-
flavored gelatin
1 orange, seeded and peeled
(white membrane removed)
Rind of 1 orange
1 can (1 pound) whole
cranberry sauce

Put ¼ cup cold water into Sunbeam Blender. Add gelatin and 1 cup boiling water. Cover and process at Stir until dissolved. Remove Feeder Cap and add orange and rind. Process at Mince until rind is finely chopped. Remove cover and add cranberry sauce, processing only until blended. Pour into 1-quart mold. Chill until firm. Unmold onto bed of greens.

CELERY REMOULADE
4 servings

2 bunches celery hearts
2 tablespoons lemon juice
2½ teaspoons salt, divided
4 tablespoons Dijon prepared
mustard

Recipe books for new Blenders and Mixers
contain information on speed settings for
other models in front, Instruction Section.

89

⅓ cup olive oil
2 to 3 tablespoons white wine
vinegar
⅓ teaspoon white pepper
Salad greens
3 tablespoons minced parsley
2 teaspoons minced chives

Wash and dry celery. Cut into small julienne strips. Place in a bowl, add lemon juice and 2 teaspoons salt. Mix well and let stand at room temperature 1 hour. To make dressing, warm the large bowl of Mixmaster Mixer by rinsing with hot water; dry. Place mustard in bowl. Turn to No. 4 and add 3 tablespoons boiling water, a few drops at a time. Continue to beat, adding the oil, 1 or 2 drops at a time. Add 2 tablespoons vinegar, ½ teaspoon salt and the pepper. Taste; add remaining vinegar and more seasoning if necessary. Mix dressing gently with marinated celery. Cover; refrigerate overnight. When ready to serve, place salad greens on four salad plates, divide celery among the plates, sprinkle with parsley and chives.

BALKAN CUCUMBERS
4 to 6 servings

2 cups unflavored yogurt
½ garlic clove, mashed
1 tablespoon white vinegar
1½ teaspoons salt
1 tablespoon olive oil
1 tablespoon snipped chives

1 teaspoon chopped mint leaves
(or ½ teaspoon dried)
1½ cups peeled, seeded, diced
cucumber
1 cup seedless green grape
halves

Place yogurt in large Mixmaster Mixer bowl. Beat at No. 6 until very smooth. Add garlic, vinegar, salt, olive oil, chives and mint leaves; beat ½ minute. Fold in cucumber and grape halves. Refrigerate at least 1 hour before serving. Serve in salad bowls.

CUCUMBER MOUSSE
8 servings

1 large or 2 small cucumbers
1 envelope unflavored gelatin
6 tablespoons mayonnaise
1 teaspoon Worcestershire
sauce
1 teaspoon salt
Dash white pepper
1 cup creamed cottage cheese

Peel cucumber and cut into 1-inch pieces. Put into Sunbeam Blender; cover and process at Puree until smooth. Reserve 1½ cups processed cucumber. Soften gelatin in ¼ cup cold water in Blender; add 2 tablespoons boiling water. Cover and process at Stir until dissolved. Add 1½ cups cucumber and remaining ingredients. Process at Mix until smooth. If desired, tint the mixture a pale green with a few drops of food coloring. Pour into a 1-quart mold or into 8 individual molds. Cover and freeze. Defrost before serving.

FROZEN PEACH-PECAN SALAD
8 servings

1 cup heavy cream, whipped
1 cup mayonnaise
2 packages (3 ounces each)
cream cheese, cubed
1 cup pecans
8 peach halves

Place cream in Sunbeam Blender. Cover and process at Whip; empty into large bowl. Put mayonnaise into Blender; gradually add cheese, processing at Mix until smooth. Stop Blender and add pecans; cover and process at Chop a few seconds. Fold the blended mixture into the whipped cream. Arrange peach halves, hollow-side up, in refrigerator tray. Pour the cheese and cream mixture over the peach halves. Cover tightly, freeze until firm.

HOT GERMAN POTATO SALAD
6 servings

6 potatoes
½ pound bacon, diced

1 onion, diced
1 tablespoon flour
½ cup vinegar
1 teaspoon salt
½ teaspoon pepper
1 tablespoon sugar
1 teaspoon Angostura bitters

Boil potatoes until tender. Peel and cube. Set aside. Preheat Multi-Cooker Frypan to 340°. Fry bacon in hot Frypan until brown and crisp. Remove bacon bits. Sauté onion in hot bacon fat until tender. Stir in flour. Mix vinegar, ½ cup water, salt, pepper and sugar. Add gradually to flour mixture in Frypan, stirring constantly over low heat. Add bitters and cook a few minutes until smooth and glossy. Turn dial to Simmer. Add cooked potatoes and bacon bits. Heat thoroughly. Serve warm.

LIME-CHEESE SALAD
8 to 10 servings

1 cup pecans or walnuts
1 cup maraschino cherries,
drained
1 cup pineapple chunks, drained
1 package (3 ounces) lime-
flavored gelatin
1 envelope unflavored gelatin
1 cup creamed cottage cheese
Few drops green food coloring
1 cup crushed ice

Place nuts, cherries and pineapple in Sunbeam Blender. Cover and process at Chop. Reserve. Put gelatins and 1 cup boiling

Recipe books for new Blenders and Mixers
contain information on speed settings for
other models in front, Instruction Section.

91

water into Blender; cover and process at Stir until dissolved. Add cottage cheese. Cover and process at Mix until smooth and an even color. Add food coloring if desired. Add 1 cup crushed ice and blend until mixture begins to thicken. Set in refrigerator 5 to 10 minutes. Pour over fruit and nuts, stir to blend. Let set a few minutes. Stir again to distribute fruit and nuts. Pour into a 2-quart mold. Refrigerate at least 1 hour before serving.

CRANBERRY DREAM SALAD
8 to 10 servings

1 cup heavy cream
1 cup crushed pineapple, drained
1 can (1 pound) whole cranberry sauce, cut up
2 tablespoons mayonnaise
2 tablespoons sugar
2 packages (3 ounces each) cream cheese, quartered
¾ cup walnuts
Lettuce

Place cream in Sunbeam Blender, cover and process at Whip. Remove to large mixing bowl and add pineapple to cream. Put cranberry sauce into Blender; cover and process at Mix until smooth. Add mayonnaise, sugar and cheese and con-

tinue to process until well blended. Add nuts and process only until chopped. Fold into whipped cream and pineapple. Pour into tray and freeze. To serve, let stand at room temperature for 15 minutes and turn out on lettuce. Slice.

IMPERIAL VALLEY BLUE CHEESE DRESSING
2½ cups

½ cup sour cream
2 tablespoons wine vinegar
½ cup buttermilk
½ teaspoon salt
¼ teaspoon white pepper
½ cup salad oil
1 package (8 ounces) blue cheese
1 clove garlic, cut up

Place all ingredients into Sunbeam Blender. Cover and process at Mix until mixture is smooth.

FRUIT DRESSING
¾ cup

½ cup salad oil
¼ cup fresh lemon juice
2 tablespoons honey
1 teaspoon salt

Put all ingredients into Sunbeam Blender. Cover and process at

Whip until blended. Good with fresh or canned fruit.

CREAMY GARLIC DRESSING
2 cups

¼ cup lemon juice
¾ cup salad oil
⅔ cup light cream
2 cloves garlic
1 teaspoon salt
½ teaspoon sugar
¼ teaspoon white pepper
½ teaspoon paprika

Put all ingredients into Sunbeam Blender; cover and process at Whip until blended.

OLD-FASHIONED SALAD DRESSING
2½ cups

1 teaspoon salt
3 teaspoons dry mustard
1 teaspoon powdered onion
4 teaspoons flour
4 tablespoons sugar
2 large eggs
⅔ cup cider vinegar
1 cup light cream
1 tablespoon softened butter
or margarine
Salt, pepper

Combine first 5 ingredients in small Mixmaster Mixer bowl. Add eggs. Beat at No. 6 until

completely blended. Turn Mixer to No. 1; beat in vinegar, then cream. Transfer to heavy saucepan and cook over low heat, stirring constantly until thickened. Remove from heat and stir in butter. Season to taste with salt, pepper. Refrigerate.

BLUE CHEESE OR ROQUEFORT DRESSING
2 cups

1 cup evaporated milk,
undiluted
½ cup salad oil
¼ cup vinegar
½ teaspoon salt
Dash garlic powder
½ cup crumbled blue or
Roquefort cheese

Place all ingredients into Sunbeam Blender; cover and process at Mix until mixture is smooth.

BLENDER MAYONNAISE
1½ cups

1 egg
2 tablespoons lemon juice
1 piece lemon rind
½ teaspoon dry mustard
1 teaspoon salt
1 cup salad oil

Place egg and lemon juice in Sunbeam Blender. Using a vegetable peeler, cut off a strip of

Recipe books for new Blenders and Mixers contain information on speed settings for other models in front, Instruction Section.

93

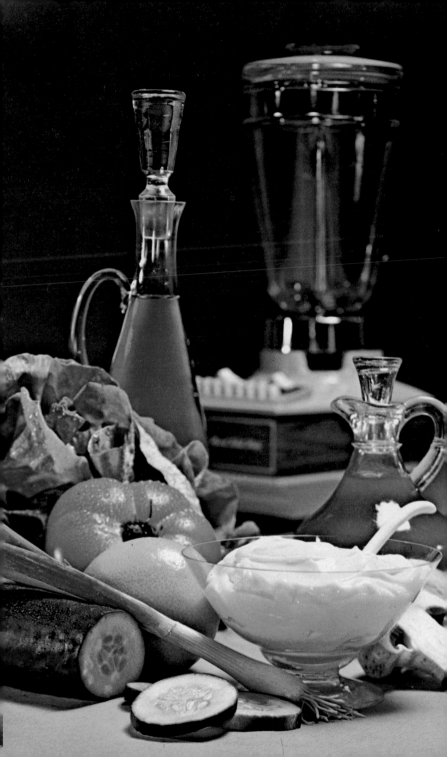

lemon rind. Add to Blender along with mustard, salt and ¼ cup oil. Cover, process at Crush 6 seconds. Remove Feeder Cap, add remaining oil in a thin stream. Turn off Blender; serve at once or refrigerate.

Try it this way: For Tarragon Mayonnaise, omit lemon juice and rind, substitute 2 tablespoons tarragon vinegar. For Tomato Mayonnaise, add 2 tablespoons tomato paste, with egg and lemon juice, an extra ¼ teaspoon salt, ¼ teaspoon white pepper. For Curry Mayonnaise, substitute 2 tablespoons cider vinegar for lemon juice and rind; add 1 teaspoon curry powder before processing.

LIME HONEY FRUIT DRESSING
1 cup

1 piece lime peel, ½ by 1 inch
⅓ cup lime juice
⅓ cup honey
¼ teaspoon salt
¾ cup salad oil
½ teaspoon paprika
¾ teaspoon prepared mustard
½ teaspoon seasoned salt

Put all ingredients into Sunbeam Blender. Cover and process at Grate until lime peel is grated.

BASIC FRENCH DRESSING
2 cups

1½ cups salad oil
⅓ cup vinegar
½ teaspoon sugar
1½ teaspoons salt
¼ teaspoon pepper
1 teaspoon paprika
½ teaspoon dry mustard

Put all ingredients into Sunbeam Blender; cover and process at Whip until well blended. Chill.

CELERY SEED DRESSING
1 cup

½ cup salad oil
1 teaspoon salt
¼ cup vinegar
½ cup honey
½ teaspoon celery seed

Put all ingredients into Sunbeam Blender; cover and process at Whip until well blended.

ANCHOVY DRESSING
1½ cups

1 cup evaporated milk
½ cup salad oil
¼ cup wine vinegar
1 teaspoon salt

Recipe books for new Blenders and Mixers contain information on speed settings for other models in front, Instruction Section.

95

¼ teaspoon pepper
Dash of garlic salt
¼ cup chopped parsley
1 can (2 ounces) anchovies

Put all ingredients into Sunbeam Blender; cover and process at Crush until smooth. Chill.

AVOCADO DRESSING
1¼ cups

½ cup orange juice
½ lemon, peeled and seeded
¼ teaspoon salt
2 teaspoons mayonnaise
1 avocado, cubed

Put all ingredients into Sunbeam Blender; cover and process at Blend until smooth. Serve on lettuce and tomato salad.

LOW CALORIE DRESSING
1 cup

1 can (8 ounces) tomato sauce
2 tablespoons tarragon vinegar
1 teaspoon Worcestershire sauce
1 teaspoon onion juice
1 teaspoon dillseed
½ teaspoon salt
½ teaspoon basil
¼ teaspoon sugar
⅛ teaspoon pepper
⅛ teaspoon oregano

Put all ingredients in Sunbeam Blender; cover and process at Whip until well blended.

APRICOT-HONEY DRESSING
2 cups

1 can (1 pound) apricots,
drained
¼ lemon, seeded and peeled
1 thin piece lemon rind,
1 by 2 inches
¼ cup honey
¼ teaspoon salt
1 cup sour cream

Put apricots, lemon and rind into Sunbeam Blender; cover and process at Whip until apricots are puréed. Add honey, salt and sour cream; cover and process only until well mixed.

THOUSAND ISLAND DRESSING
1½ cups

1 cup mayonnaise
¼ cup chili sauce
1 teaspoon Worcestershire sauce
½ glove garlic
2 tablespoons pickle relish
2 1-inch squares green pepper
2 teaspoons cut chives
2 hard-cooked eggs, quartered

Put mayonnaise, chili sauce,

Worcestershire sauce and garlic into Sunbeam Blender. Cover and process at Whip until well blended. Stop Blender and add remaining ingredients; cover and process at Chop only until pepper is coarsely chopped.

 or

QUICK HOLLANDAISE SAUCE
¾ cup

½ cup butter or margarine
1 egg
2 tablespoons lemon juice
¼ teaspoon salt
Pinch cayenne pepper

Melt butter in top of double boiler over hot, *not boiling,* water. Add egg, lemon juice, salt and cayenne. Beat with Mixmaster Hand Mixer or Mixmaster Mixer removed from stand, until mixture is thick and smooth. Remove at once from hot water. Serve warm over vegetables.

SWEET-SOUR BASTING SAUCE
1 cup

2 tablespoons salad oil
1 teaspoon salt
⅛ green pepper
1 can (6 ounces) frozen pineapple juice concentrate
½ clove garlic

⅓ cup brown sugar
½ cup wine vinegar
1 teaspoon soy sauce
½ jar (2 ounces) pimiento
Pineapple chunks and green pepper strips

Put all ingredients except pineapple chunks and green pepper strips into Sunbeam Blender; cover and process at Mix until thoroughly blended. Brush on pork or chicken while it broils, roasts or barbecues. Add a few pineapple chunks and green pepper strips for garnish.

WESTERN BARBECUE SAUCE
2½ cups

1 bottle (14 ounces) tomato ketchup
½ cup undiluted consommé
¼ cup wine vinegar
2 tablespoons soy sauce
1 tablespoon brown sugar
⅛ teaspoon garlic powder
½ teaspoon salt
⅓ cup salad oil

Put all ingredients into Sunbeam Blender; cover and process at Mix until well blended. Pour into saucepan and heat. Use for basting chicken, steak or chops of any kind, or fish, during barbecuing.

Recipe books for new Blenders and Mixers contain information on speed settings for other models in front, Instruction Section.

97

BEARNAISE SAUCE
2 cups

1 cup dry white wine
2 tablespoons tarragon vinegar
4 sprigs parsley
3 shallots or onion slices
1 teaspoon tarragon
1 teaspoon chervil
2 peppercorns
¾ cup Hollandaise sauce
(page 97)

Mix all ingredients except Hollandaise in saucepan; bring to a boil and cook until reduced to ⅔ volume. Remove peppercorns. Pour mixture into Sunbeam Blender; add Hollandaise; cover and process at Grate until well blended. Serve on meat or fish.

FRESH HORSERADISH SAUCE
1½ cups

1 cup horseradish root, cut into
½-inch cubes
¾ cup white vinegar
1 to 2 tablespoons sugar
¼ teaspoon salt

Put all ingredients into Sunbeam Blender; cover and process at Grate until finely grated.

LEMON PARSLEY SAUCE
½ cup

½ cup parsley sprigs
1 medium onion, quartered
1 lemon, peeled, seeded and
quartered
½ teaspoon salt

Put all ingredients into Sunbeam Blender. Process at Mince until smooth. Brush on fish while baking, broiling or barbecuing.

SAUCE VERTE
2 cups

¼ cup oil
½ cup washed spinach leaves
½ cup parsley sprigs
1 clove garlic
2 tablespoons chives
1¼ cups mayonnaise

Put all ingredients except mayonnaise into Sunbeam Blender; cover and process at Chop until vegetables are very finely chopped and mixture is bright green. Fold into mayonnaise.

BREADS AND OTHER BAKED TREATS

Is there any smell better than that of baking bread? Here are many ways to fill your home with that appetizing odor and delight your family with the result. Pancakes here, too, and waffles, spoon bread, hush puppies—surprises of many kinds for family and friends, all courtesy of your love for cooking, and the make-it-quickly help of your Sunbeam Appliances.

SUNDAY BRUNCH COFFEE CAKE
16 servings

¼ cup butter or margarine
1 cup sugar
2 eggs
1½ cups plus 2 tablespoons cake flour, sifted
¼ teaspoon salt
2¾ teaspoons baking powder
½ cup milk
1 tablespoon butter, melted
3 tablespoons sugar
½ cup chopped walnuts

Preheat oven to 350° F. Place butter and 1 cup sugar in large bowl of Mixmaster Mixer. With Dial set at No. 7, cream until fluffy. Sift dry ingredients together. Add to butter mixture alternately with milk, with Dial set at No. 1. Pour into a greased 8-inch square pan. Spread melted butter over top. Sprinkle with 3 tablespoons sugar and the walnuts. Bake 45 minutes. Cut in squares and serve hot.

CHEESE MUFFINS
1 dozen

2 cups sifted flour
4 teaspoons baking powder
1 tablespoon sugar
½ teaspoon salt
1 egg
1 cup milk
3 tablespoons soft butter or margarine
½ pound sharp Cheddar cheese, cubed

Preheat oven to 350° F. Grease muffin tins well. Sift flour, baking powder, sugar and salt into large bowl of Mixmaster Mixer. Put egg, milk and butter into Sunbeam Blender, cover and process at Mix until smooth. Remove Feeder Cap, add Cheddar, process at Chop only until Cheddar is finely chopped. Pour into dry ingredients. Set Dial at No. 1. Mix only until flour is moistened. Fill prepared tins ⅔ full. Bake 15 to 25 minutes.

Recipe books for new Blenders and Mixers
contain information on speed settings for
other models in front, Instruction Section.

99

SPOON BREAD
6 servings

2 cups milk
½ cup cornmeal
1 teaspoon salt
½ teaspoon baking powder
½ teaspoon sugar
2 tablespoons melted butter
or margarine
3 eggs, separated

Preheat oven to 375° F. Scald milk; add cornmeal and cook until thick. Stir in salt, baking powder, sugar and butter. Put egg yolks into small bowl of Mixmaster Mixer and egg whites into large bowl. With Dial set at No. 12, beat whites until stiff. Reserve. With Dial set at No. 5, beat yolks. Stir yolks into cornmeal mixture. With Dial set at No. 1, fold cornmeal mixture into beaten whites. Pour into a well-buttered 1½-quart casserole and bake, uncovered, 25 to 30 minutes.

POPOVERS
8 to 10

2 eggs
1 cup milk
1 cup sifted flour
¼ teaspoon salt

Preheat oven to 450° F. Put all ingredients into Sunbeam Blender. Cover and process at Mix until perfectly smooth. Fill well-greased muffin tins, custard cups or popover pans half full. Bake 10 minutes. Reduce heat to 350° and bake 35 minutes longer. (For higher popovers, heat pans before filling.)

QUICK BASIC MUFFINS
1 dozen

2 cups sifted all-purpose flour
¼ cup sugar
¾ teaspoon salt
3 teaspoons baking powder
1 egg
1 cup milk
¼ cup melted shortening, butter
or bacon drippings, cooled

Preheat oven to 425° F. Sift together into large Mixmaster Mixer bowl flour, sugar, salt and baking powder. Add egg, milk and shortening. Beat at No. 3 about 30 seconds, only enough to mix, scraping bowl. Fill greased muffin pans ⅔ full. Bake about 20 minutes.

BAKING POWDER
BISCUITS
1½ dozens

2 cups sifted all-purpose flour
1 teaspoon salt
3 teaspoons baking powder
⅓ cup soft shortening or butter
¾ cup milk (about)

Preheat oven to 450° F. Sift

flour, salt and baking powder into large Mixmaster Mixer bowl. Add shortening; beat at No. 1 speed about 1½ minutes or until consistency of coarse meal. Pour in milk, adding just enough to form a soft dough. Beat about 30 seconds, only long enough to mix. Turn out onto lightly floured surface. Knead gently, folding over a few times to even texture. Pat or roll ½ to ¾ inch thick. Cut with floured cutter or cut into squares with a knife. Place on ungreased baking sheet—far apart for crusty sides or close together for soft sides. Bake 12 to 15 minutes or until brown. Serve piping hot with plenty of butter.

OATMEAL NUT BREAD
1 loaf

1½ cups sifted flour
½ teaspoon salt
½ teaspoon baking powder
1 teaspoon baking soda
¾ cup quick-cooking oatmeal
1 egg
½ cup sugar
1 cup sour cream
⅓ cup dark molasses
½ cup pitted dates
1 cup nuts

Preheat oven to 350° F. Line a greased 8½- by 4½-inch loaf pan with wax paper; grease again. Sift flour, salt, baking powder and soda into mixing bowl. Add oatmeal. Put egg,

sugar, sour cream and molasses into Sunbeam Blender; cover and process at Mix until smooth and well blended. Add dates and nuts and process at Chop until dates are chopped. Empty into dry ingredients and stir well. Fill prepared pan and bake 45 to 55 minutes.

ORANGE-DATE LOAF
1 loaf

2 cups sifted flour
2 teaspoons baking powder
½ teaspoon salt
1 egg
2 tablespoons shortening
¾ cup sugar
¾ cup orange juice
1 piece orange rind, ½ inch
by 2 inches
½ teaspoon almond extract
½ cup nutmeats
½ cup pitted dates

Preheat oven to 350° F. Grease an 8½- by 4½-inch loaf pan. Sift flour, baking powder and salt into a large bowl of Mixmaster Mixer. Put egg, shortening, sugar, orange juice and rind into Sunbeam Blender; cover and blend at Mix until smooth. Stop Blender, add extract, nuts and dates; cover and process at Chop only until nuts and dates are chopped. Pour mixture over dry ingredients. Turn Dial to No. 1; mix only until dry ingre-

Recipe books for new Blenders and Mixers
contain information on speed settings for
other models in front, Instruction Section.   101

dients are moistened. Turn into greased pan. Bake for 55 to 60 minutes.

STOVEPIPE BREAD
2 small loaves

3½ cups sifted flour, divided
1 package active-dry yeast
½ cup milk
½ cup salad oil
¼ cup sugar
1 teaspoon salt
2 eggs

Measure 1½ cups of the sifted flour into large bowl of Mixmaster Mixer. Add yeast and blend at No. 3 speed ½ minute. Combine milk, ½ cup water, oil, sugar and salt in a small saucepan. Heat on low heat until mixture is just warm. Add to dry ingredients in the Mixer bowl and beat at No. 3 speed until smooth. Add eggs and beat at No. 4 speed until mixture is blended. Turn to No. 1 speed and gradually add 1 cup flour. Beat until smooth and well blended. Scrape beaters. Remove bowl and stir in remaining 1 cup flour with a spoon to make a soft dough. Spoon batter into two wellgreased 1-pound coffee cans. Cover with the plastic lids and let stand in a warm place, free from draft. When dough has risen almost to top of cans, remove lids. Bake in preheated

375° F. oven 30 to 35 minutes or until browned. Let cool about 10 minutes in cans before removing to cooling racks.

BRAN MUFFINS
1 dozen

1 cup sifted flour
2½ teaspoons baking powder
½ teaspoon salt
1 egg
2 tablespoons soft shortening
¼ cup sugar
¾ cup milk
1 cup bran

Preheat oven to 400° F. Sift flour, baking powder and salt into large bowl of Mixmaster Mixer. Put egg, shortening, sugar, milk and bran into Sunbeam Blender. Cover and process at Mix until blended. Pour mixture over dry ingredients in Mixer bowl. Beat at No. 3 speed about 30 seconds, just enough to mix ingredients. Fill greased muffin tins ⅔ full. Bake 20 to 25 minutes or until browned.

CRANBERRY-NUT LOAF
1 loaf

2 cups sifted flour
1½ teaspoons baking powder
½ teaspoon soda
1 egg
¼ cup shortening

Recipe books for new Blenders and Mixers contain information on speed settings for other models in front, Instruction Section.

103

1 teaspoon salt
1 piece orange rind,
1 inch by 2 inches
1 cup sugar
¾ cup orange juice
½ cup nuts
1 cup cranberries

Preheat oven to 350° F. Grease loaf pan. Sift flour, baking powder and soda into large bowl of Mixmaster Mixer. Put egg, shortening, salt, orange rind, sugar and orange juice into Sunbeam Blender. Cover and process at Grate until rind is finely grated. Add nuts and cranberries and process only until chopped. Empty into flour mixture. Turn Dial to No. 1; mix only until blended. Spoon into prepared pan. Bake 50 to 60 minutes or until cake tester inserted comes out clean.

PEANUT BUTTER ORANGE BREAD
1 loaf

¾ cup peanut butter
½ cup butter or margarine
2 cups sifted all-purpose flour
½ cup sugar
1½ teaspoons baking powder
1 teaspoon salt
½ teaspoon baking soda
1 tablespoon grated orange rind
1 egg, beaten
1 cup milk

Preheat oven to 350° F. In large Mixmaster Mixer bowl, cream together peanut butter and butter at No. 7 until light and fluffy. Sift flour, sugar, baking powder and salt together into creamed mixture and beat at No. 1 one minute or until crumbs form. Add orange rind, egg and milk; beat at No. 3 until all of mixture is moistened. Pour into greased 9- by 5-inch loaf pan. Bake 55 minutes or until cake tester inserted in center comes out clean. Remove from pan. Cool before slicing.

ORANGE PECAN WAFFLES
8 servings

1½ cups sifted cake flour
2½ teaspoons baking powder
½ teaspoon salt
2 tablespoons sugar
2 eggs, separated
2 tablespoons grated orange
rind
½ cup orange juice
½ cup milk
⅓ cup melted butter or
margarine, cooled
½ cup chopped pecans

Sift together flour, baking powder, salt and sugar. Beat egg whites in small Mixmaster Mixer bowl at highest speed until stiff but still moist. Beat yolks in large Mixmaster Mixer bowl at highest speed until thick. Add orange rind, juice and milk. Beat until blended, then add dry ingredients and beat at No. 3 just until blended. Beat in melted butter and pecans, scraping bowl, then fold in beaten egg whites at No. 1. Bake on preheated Sunbeam Waffle Baker and Grill set at Medium. Stir batter each time before pouring.

WAFFLES
16 servings

3 cups sifted all-purpose flour
5 teaspoons baking powder
1 teaspoon salt
2 tablespoons sugar
4 large eggs
2¼ cups milk
1½ teaspoons vanilla, if
desired
⅔ cup melted butter or
margarine, cooled

Sift together in large bowl of Mixmaster Mixer flour, baking powder, salt and sugar. Put eggs into small Mixmaster Mixer bowl and beat at highest speed 1 minute. Add milk and vanilla to beaten eggs, then add mixture to dry ingredients. Beat at No. 4 about 1½ minutes until blended. Add butter; beat at No. 2 only until blended. Use measuring pitcher for easy pouring, or pour from 8-ounce measuring cup. Bake on preheated Sunbeam Waffle Baker and Grill at Medium.

Blueberry Waffles: Sprinkle drained fresh or frozen blueberries over unbaked batter in Waffle Baker. Bake as directed.

Apple Waffles: Fold 3½ cups pared and coarsely grated raw apples into basic waffle batter. Sift 1 teaspoon cinnamon with dry ingredients. Extra good with ham.

Cheese Waffles: Add 1½ cups grated process American cheese to basic recipe before adding butter. Delicious when topped with creamed ham and mushrooms or creamed vegetables.

SCOTCH CREAM SCONES
16 scones

2 cups sifted flour
¾ teaspoon salt
1 teaspoon sugar
1 teaspoon baking powder
1 teaspoon soda
1 cup sour cream
5 tablespoons butter or
margarine
1 cup currants

Sift together flour, salt, sugar and baking powder in large bowl of Mixmaster Mixer. Combine soda, 2 tablespoons water and sour cream in small bowl of Mixer; beat at No. 6. Add butter to flour mixture in large bowl. Beat at No. 2 speed until mixture is like cornmeal. Add sour cream mixture and beat only until blended. Stir in currants. Turn out onto a lightly floured board and knead slightly. Divide dough into four parts. Pat each part into a circle 1 inch thick.

Recipe books for new Blenders and Mixers contain information on speed settings for other models in front, Instruction Section.

105

Cut circles in quarters. Heat Sunbeam Griddle to 300°. Grease lightly. Cook dough slowly on hot Griddle, about 20 minutes, turning frequently for even browning on both sides.

GRIDDLE CAKES
2 dozens

2 cups sifted flour
3 teaspoons baking powder
1 teaspoon salt
2 tablespoons sugar
1 egg
1½ cups milk
3 tablespoons melted butter
or margarine

Sift together flour, baking powder, salt and sugar into large bowl of Mixmaster Mixer. Put egg into small bowl of Mixer and beat at No. 12 speed, 1 minute. Add milk and beat at No. 6, 15 seconds. Pour over dry ingredients. Beat at No. 1 speed until just blended, about 1 minute, scraping bowl with rubber scraper. Quickly blend in melted butter. Preheat Sunbeam Griddle or Multi-Cooker Frypan to 400°. Drop by spoonfuls onto heated Griddle, turning only once to brown both sides. Serve immediately.

Pecan Griddle Cakes: Add ¾ to 1 cup finely chopped pecans to batter, blend in. Serve with whipped cream or ice cream.

Banana Griddle Cakes: Bake at 380°. Before turning griddle cakes, put 3 or 4 thin slices banana on each. Turn and finish baking. Serve with butter, sugar and cinnamon or sugar mixed with grated lemon peel.

Blueberry Griddle Cakes: Before turning griddle cakes, sprinkle a few fresh or unthawed frozen blueberries over each. Serve with soft butter and honey.

SUGARY SPICE PUFFS
3 dozens

4 tablespoons butter or
margarine, softened
1¼ cups sugar, divided
1 egg
1 teaspoon grated lemon peel
2 cups sifted all-purpose flour
4 teaspoons baking powder
½ teaspoon salt
¼ teaspoon nutmeg
1 cup milk
2 teaspoons ginger
½ cup butter or margarine,
melted

Preheat oven to 375° F. In large Mixmaster Mixer bowl with Dial set at No. 7, cream softened butter with ½ cup sugar. Beat in egg and lemon peel. Sift flour with baking powder, salt and nutmeg. Add alternately with milk to butter mixture, beating briefly after each addition. Spoon into greased 2-inch muffin cups. Bake 15 minutes. Mix ginger with remaining sugar. While muffins are hot, dip each in butter, then in sugar mixture.

Recipe books for new Blenders and Mixers
contain information on speed settings for
other models in front, Instruction Section.

DOUGHNUT PUFFS
2½ dozens

2 tablespoons butter or
margarine
½ cup sugar
2 eggs
2 cups sifted flour
2 teaspoons baking powder
½ teaspoon salt
¼ teaspoon nutmeg
½ teaspoon mace
½ cup milk
Shortening or salad oil for frying
Sugar

Cream butter and sugar together in large bowl of Mixmaster Mixer at No. 7 speed. Add eggs and beat well. Sift together flour, baking powder, salt, nutmeg and mace. Set Mixer at No. 1 speed. Add flour mixture and milk alternately, mixing to make a smooth, soft dough. Chill dough thoroughly. Heat fat in Sunbeam Cooker and Deep Fryer to 375°. Drop dough by rounded spoonfuls into hot fat, dipping spoon into hot fat each time before putting into batter. Fry until golden brown, turning to brown evenly, about 3 minutes. Lift basket to drain supports. Drain. Put puffs on paper towels. Roll in sugar before serving.

Serving style: Fry these "to order" for a Halloween party, serve piping hot with glasses of cold cider.

LEMON MUFFINS
2 dozens

4 eggs, separated
1 cup butter or margarine
1 cup sugar
2 cups flour
2 teaspoons baking powder
1 teaspoon salt
½ cup lemon juice
2 teaspoons grated lemon peel

Preheat oven to 375° F. Place egg whites in small bowl of Mixmaster Mixer. With Dial set at No. 12, beat until stiff. Reserve. Place butter in large bowl of Mixmaster Mixer. With Dial set at No. 7, cream until fluffy. Add egg yolks, one at a time, beating until fluffy after each addition. Sift together sugar, flour, baking powder and salt. With Dial set at No. 1, add dry ingredients to butter-egg mixture alternately with lemon juice, mixing briefly after each addition. Fold in egg whites and lemon peel. Fill greased muffin pans ¾ full. Bake about 20 minutes.

Good to know: These freeze nicely. If you have leftovers, split, toast and butter them.

COOK-AT-TABLE SPECIALS

When you are the proud owner of Sunbeam portable appliances, a whole new world of cook-serve-and-eat ideas opens up to you. Although many of the recipes in this book can be used for at-table cooking, the ones in this section are particularly adapted to it—to cooking with flair and to serving with style any meal of the day for any family or company occasion.

SWISS EGGS
4 servings

2 tablespoons butter or
margarine
1 cup light cream
8 eggs
Salt
Tabasco sauce
Bread slices
1 cup grated Swiss cheese
3 tablespoons sherry

Melt butter in Multi-Cooker Frypan set at 300°. Add cream and heat until bubbling. Break eggs into cream; season each with salt and a dash of Tabasco. Reduce heat to 260° and cook eggs until whites are nearly set. Meanwhile toast bread in Sunbeam Toaster and butter it. Sprinkle cheese over eggs and cook until whites are set. Remove eggs to toast slices. Add sherry to cream in Frypan; cook 30 seconds. Pour over eggs on toast. If desired, sprinkle with slivered, toasted almonds.

SUNDAY BREAKFAST EGGS
4 servings

6 eggs
1 package (3 ounces) cream
cheese
1 cup milk, scalded
1 cup diced cooked ham
2 tablespoons butter or
margarine

Place eggs in large bowl of Mixmaster Mixer. Beat at No. 3 just until well blended. Reserve. Place cheese in small bowl of Mixmaster Mixer. Beat at No. 3 until fluffy. Gradually beat in milk. Add to eggs and beat just until blended. Stir in ham; season to taste. At table: Heat Multi-Cooker Frypan to 300°. Melt butter. Pour in egg mixture. Cook, stirring until eggs are set.

Serving style: For a brunch party, double the recipe above. Serve with broiled grapefruit, hot Scones (page 105) and Sunday Coffee Cake (page 99).

Recipe books for new Blenders and Mixers
contain information on speed settings for
other models in front, Instruction Section.

109

BRUNCH OMELET
4 servings

6 eggs
⅓ cup milk
½ teaspoon salt
¼ teaspoon white pepper
2 tablespoons butter or
margarine
1 cup creamed cottage cheese
1 tablespoon chopped chives
1 tablespoon minced green
pepper
Tomato wedges
Watercress sprigs

With Dial set at lowest speed, beat eggs with Mixmaster Hand Mixer just until well blended. Beat in milk, salt and pepper. Melt butter in Multi-Cooker Frypan set at 300°. Pour in omelet mixture. As it cooks, run spatula around edges to allow uncooked portion to flow underneath. While eggs cook, mix together cheese, chives and green pepper. When eggs are just cooked and still shiny on surface, loosen edges all around. Place cheese mixture in center of omelet. Roll omelet over mixture and transfer to a warm platter. Surround with tomato and watercress.

ITALIAN BRUNCH
6 servings

½ pound Italian sweet sausage
2 tablespoons olive oil
1 cup peeled, diced potatoes
½ cup thin-sliced onion
¼ cup chopped green pepper
1 cup peeled, seeded, diced
tomatoes
8 eggs
¼ cup cream
Salt, pepper

In Multi-Cooker Frypan, heated to 325°, sauté sausage in olive oil until sausage is no longer pink. Add potatoes, onion and green pepper and cook, stirring occasionally until potatoes are brown and onion and pepper are limp. Add tomatoes, cook 1 minute. With Mixmaster Hand Mixer set at medium speed, lightly beat eggs, cream, dash each of salt and pepper together. Pour into Frypan. Reduce heat to 260° and cook, stirring until eggs are set but still moist. **Serving style:** Serve these dressed-up eggs on thick slices of Italian bread, toasted. Sprinkle with oregano and grated Romano cheese for a perfect company-coming Sunday brunch.

FARMERS' BREAKFAST
4 servings

6 slices bacon, diced
½ cup diced green pepper
¼ cup minced onion
1½ cups diced cooked potatoes
Salt, pepper
6 eggs
½ cup milk or light cream
Paprika

110

Place bacon in cold Multi-Cooker Frypan. Turn Dial to 300° and fry bacon until browned. Pour off all but about 3 tablespoons bacon drippings. Add green pepper and onion, and sauté 5 minutes. Add potatoes and cook until light brown, stirring occasionally. Sprinkle with salt and pepper. Beat eggs with milk, just enough to blend; season with salt and pepper. Pour eggs into pan over vegetables. Cook, stirring lightly until eggs are set but still moist and creamy. Sprinkle with paprika.

Serving style: Start Sunday breakfast with lots of freshly squeezed orange juice. Serve Farmers' Breakfast, hot Stovepipe Bread (page 103) with strawberry jam; coffee for the grownups, milk for the children.

SCRAMBLED EGGS WITH WATER CHESTNUTS
4 to 6 servings
6 eggs
½ teaspoon salt
½ cup sour cream
2 tablespoons butter or
margarine
¼ cup chopped water chestnuts

Using Mixmaster Hand Mixer set at medium speed, beat eggs 1 minute. Add salt, ¼ cup water and sour cream; beat 30 seconds. Heat Multi-Cooker Frypan to 300°. Melt butter in Frypan; pour in egg mixture and cook,

stirring occasionally until eggs are thick and creamy. Add water chestnuts. Serve on toast.
Good to know: For a more substantial brunch or luncheon dish, stir in ¾ cup diced cooked shrimp with the water chestnuts.

BRUNCH EGGS
6 servings

2 medium onions, sliced
3 tablespoons butter or
margarine
3 green peppers, seeded,
thinly sliced
3 medium tomatoes, thinly
sliced
½ cup chopped parsley
½ teaspoon salt
¼ teaspoon black pepper,
coarsely ground
6 eggs
½ cup shredded Muenster
cheese

Preheat Multi-Cooker Frypan to 325°. Sauté the onions in the butter 5 minutes. Add green peppers, tomatoes and parsley and combine. Add ½ cup water, salt and pepper. Cover Frypan and cook, stirring occasionally, about 30 minutes, until all liquid has evaporated. Turn Frypan down to 300°. With the back of a tablespoon, make 6 depressions in the cooked vegetables. Break eggs individually into a saucer and slip an egg into each depression. Cook, covered, about 4 minutes. Uncover, sprinkle with

111

cheese, and cook 1 to 2 minutes longer until set.

Serving style: These are delicious served on toasted, buttered halves of English muffins. Or serve in mashed potato nests for supper.

ITALIAN RICE BALLS
2½ dozens

1½ cups grated Parmesan cheese
4 cups hot cooked rice
½ pound Mozzarella cheese
½ cup minced cooked ham
Oil for deep frying
4 eggs
1½ cups fine dry bread crumbs

Stir half of Parmesan into hot rice and let the mixture cool. Cut 30 ½-inch cubes from Mozzarella and reserve. Mince the remaining mozzarella. Mix minced Mozzarella and ham; stir two eggs and remaining Parmesan into this mixture; add to cooled rice and blend thoroughly. Form into balls, using about ¼ cup rice mixture for each. With a finger, make a small hole in each ball and poke a Mozzarella cube into the hole; reshape rice into a ball around cheese cube. Beat the remaining eggs lightly with a fork. Heat oil in Sunbeam Cooker and Deep Fryer to 400°. Roll rice balls in eggs, then in bread crumbs. Fry rice balls in deep fat until golden brown, turning to brown.

Party idea: These Italian Suppli di Riso, fried while guests watch hungrily, might be the one hot dish that graces a simple buffet. Serve cold sliced turkey and corned beef, dark pumpernickel, a selection of salads, and perhaps Dressed-Up Lemon Cake (page 135) for dessert.

DESSERT PANCAKES
12 servings

3 cups pancake flour
3 cups milk
2 eggs
¼ cup melted butter or margarine
2 cups heavy cream
½ cup confectioners sugar
3 cups honey
¼ cup lime juice

In large bowl of Mixmaster Mixer, combine first 4 ingredients. Beat at No. 2 until just well blended. Pour batter into a pretty pitcher. Wash beater and bowl; place heavy cream in bowl and beat at No. 9 until the cream forms soft peaks, gradually beating in confectioners sugar. Heat honey and lime juice together until very hot. Preheat Sunbeam Griddle or Multi-Cooker Frypan to 400° and bake pancakes, using about 3 tablespoons of mixture for each pancake. Brown on one side; turn and brown other side. As pancakes are finished, put two tablespoons sweetened cream on each; fold over and press edges lightly together. Spoon two tablespoons of hot honey-lime juice mixture over each. Two pancakes make one dessert serving.

MARMALADE DESSERT OMELETS
8 servings

4 eggs, separated
3 tablespoons sour cream
½ teaspoon salt
¼ cup flour
2 teaspoons sugar
4 tablespoons butter or margarine
Orange or lime marmalade, heated

Place egg whites in large Mixmaster Mixer bowl, yolks in small bowl. With Mixmaster Mixer at highest speed, beat whites until stiff but not dry. Reserve. With Dial set at No. 5, beat egg yolks until well blended. Beat in sour cream. Mix salt, flour and sugar. Blend into yolk-cream mixture with Dial set at No. 1. Fold in stiffly beaten whites. At table: Melt butter in Multi-Cooker Frypan set at 350°. Cook spoonfuls of egg mixture like pancakes, making thin individual omelets. Have heated marmalade ready in nearby warmer. Place omelets on serving plate, spoon marmalade over.

Serving style: Star these at brunch with Popovers (page 100).

CHERRY WAFFLE SUNDAES
8 servings

1 can (1 pound) pitted dark sweet cherries
1 can (1 pound) light sweet cherries
1 cup sugar
2 tablespoons grated orange rind
Few drops red food coloring
3 tablespoons cornstarch
¼ cup cherry liqueur
8 waffles
Vanilla ice cream

Drain cherries, reserving syrup. Pit cherries, if necessary. Place cherry syrup, sugar, orange rind and coloring in Multi-Cooker Frypan. Combine cornstarch with a little water and stir into remaining syrup in Frypan. Turn Dial to 300° and bring to a boil, stirring until mixture is thick and clear. Add cherries and heat thoroughly. Lower heat to I of Simmer and stir in cherry liqueur. Make waffles (page 105) in Sunbeam Waffle Baker and Grill. Spoon ice cream on top of waffles and cover with hot cherry sauce.

FRENCH-TOASTED POUND CAKE
5 servings

2 eggs
¼ cup milk

Recipe books for new Blenders and Mixers contain information on speed settings for other models in front, Instruction Section.

113

*1 tablespoon butter or
margarine*
5 ½-inch slices pound cake
Sour cream
Strawberry preserves
Chopped salted almonds

With Mixmaster Hand Mixer set at lowest speed, beat eggs just until blended; beat in milk until blended. Melt butter in Multi-Cooker Frypan preheated to 340°. Dip pound cake slices in egg mixture; sauté in butter until lightly browned on both sides. Top each slice with a dab of sour cream. Place a little strawberry on cream, sprinkle with almonds.

CHERRIES JUBILEE
4 to 6 servings

*1 can (27 to 29 ounces) dark
sweet cherries*
3 thin slices lemon
1 teaspoon cornstarch
¼ cup sugar
½ cup brandy, warmed
Vanilla ice cream

Put cherries, with juice, and lemon slices in Sunbeam Multi-Cooker Frypan. Set Dial at Simmer. Combine cornstarch and 2 tablespoons cold water to make smooth paste. When cherry mixture is simmering, stir in cornstarch. Cook until mixture boils and thickens slightly. Sprinkle sugar over cherries. Carefully pour warmed brandy over cherries. Ignite with a wooden match. Carefully spoon over in-

dividual servings of ice cream. **Caution:** Don't cook this—or any flamed dish—in a no-stick-surface pan; damage might result.

FRYPAN STIR-FRY CHICKEN
4 servings

2 broiler-fryer chicken breasts
1 tablespoon cornstarch
2 tablespoons soy sauce
1 teaspoon salt
*2 or 3 slices fresh ginger or
½ teaspoon powdered ginger*
¼ cup salad oil
1 small onion, sliced
¼ pound mushrooms, sliced
*½ cup blanched almonds or
walnuts*
*1 can (5 ounces) water chestnuts,
sliced*
*1 can (5 ounces) sliced bamboo
shoots with liquid*
½ cup fresh or frozen peas
Hot cooked rice

Have butcher remove bones and skins from chicken breasts. Cut into very thin strips with Sunbeam Knife. Combine cornstarch, 2 tablespoons water, soy sauce, salt and ginger. Mix well. Stir in chicken breasts. Assemble remaining ingredients, with chicken breasts, on a tray for convenience at the table. Preheat Multi-Cooker Frypan to 420° and heat oil. Add chicken, onion, mushrooms and almonds. Cook, stirring occasionally, about 3 minutes or until chicken is white.

Add water chestnuts, bamboo shoots with liquid, and peas. Cover and cook 3 minutes at low heat until mixture is heated through. Serve with hot cooked rice and additional soy sauce.

CHIPPED BEEF AND ARTICHOKES
4 servings

¼ pound chipped dried beef
1 can (14 ounces) artichoke
   hearts, drained
1 can (10½ ounces) cream of
   mushroom soup
¾ cup milk
⅛ teaspoon cayenne pepper
¼ teaspoon salt
2 tablespoons butter or
   margarine
4 slices bread

Cut chipped beef into small pieces. Cover with boiling water, let stand 1 minute. Drain thoroughly. Cut each artichoke into halves or quarters. Combine soup, milk, cayenne and salt. Assemble ingredients. At table: Preheat Multi-Cooker Frypan at 300°. Melt butter in Frypan. Add chipped beef and cook until edges begin to curl. Stir in soup mixture. Bring just to a boil. Lower heat to Simmer. Add artichoke hearts and heat thoroughly. Make toast from bread slices in a Sunbeam Toaster. Cut toast into triangles. Serve chipped beef and artichokes over toast for lunch or supper.

SEAFOOD AU GRATIN
4 servings

¾ pound scallops
¼ cup dry white wine
3 tablespoons butter or
   margarine
3 tablespoons flour
⅛ teaspoon pepper
½ teaspoon salt
1 cup milk
¼ pound American cheese,
   grated
1 cup cooked or canned lobster
   pieces
1 can (3 ounces) sliced
   mushrooms, drained
4 slices bread

Wash scallops. If large, cut into bite-sized pieces. Place in a small saucepan with ¼ cup water and white wine. Bring to a boil and cook 5 minutes. Drain, reserving liquid. Place all ingredients on a tray. Preheat Multi-Cooker Frypan to 260°. Melt butter. Stir in flour, pepper and salt. Slowly stir in milk and liquid from scallops. Cook, stirring constantly until sauce is smooth and thickened. Add cheese and stir until cheese is melted. Add scallops, lobster and mushrooms. Reduce heat to I of Simmer and heat thoroughly. Toast bread in Sunbeam Toaster. Cut into triangles. Serve hot seafood on toast.
Serving style: Frenched green beans are delicious with this dish.

CHICKEN LIVERS WITH EGGS
4 servings

½ pound chicken livers
4 hard-cooked eggs
¼ cup butter or margarine,
divided
2 tablespoons sherry
1½ tablespoons flour
¾ teaspoon salt
⅛ teaspoon pepper
1 cup milk
1 cup cooked peas
4 slices bread

Cut chicken livers into bite-sized pieces. Cut hard-cooked eggs into quarters. Assemble remaining ingredients. At table: Preheat Multi-Cooker Frypan to 320°. Melt 2 tablespoons of the butter in Frypan. Add chicken livers and cook until lightly browned. Add sherry and cook, stirring, about 3 minutes. Remove chicken livers from Frypan. Add remaining 2 tablespoons butter to Frypan. Stir in flour, salt and pepper. Slowly stir in milk. Cook at Simmer, stirring constantly until sauce is smooth and thickened. Stir in peas and browned chicken livers. Place quartered eggs over top of livers. Cover and heat at I of Simmer until eggs are warm. Toast bread in Sunbeam Toaster. Cut into triangles and serve livers over toast for brunch or a company luncheon.

CRAB A LA DEWEY
4 servings

½ cup mayonnaise
2 tablespoons flour
1 can (4 ounces) mushrooms
¼ cup milk
2 tablespoons butter or
margarine
4 scallions, chopped
1 pound cooked crab meat,
picked over
1 cup dry white wine
4 slices bread

Combine mayonnaise and flour in a small saucepan. Stir in liquid from mushrooms and milk. Cook over very low heat, stirring constantly until mixture thickens. Stir in mushrooms. Keep warm over very low heat. Melt butter in Multi-Cooker Frypan at 280°. Add scallions and cook about 5 minutes, stirring frequently. Add crab meat and wine. Turn heat to 300° and cook 5 minutes. Pour mayonnaise mixture over crab meat and mix gently. Simmer gently 5 minutes. Toast bread in Sunbeam Toaster. Serve crab meat hot over toast points.

TURKEY BREAST MARSALA
4 servings

4 tablespoons butter or
margarine

8 slices cooked turkey breast,
  about ¼ inch thick
Dash freshly ground pepper
8 thin slices prosciutto
1 package (8 ounces)
Mozzarella cheese, cut into 8
  slices
½ cup Marsala
Snipped parsley

Preheat Multi-Cooker Frypan to 300°. Melt butter in hot Frypan. Sauté turkey slices until golden brown on each side, about 1 minute. Add more butter if needed. Remove turkey slices as they brown, and set aside. Lower heat to Simmer. Return slices to Frypan, overlapping. Sprinkle with pepper. Place a slice of ham and one of cheese on each slice of turkey. Pour Marsala over top. Cover and simmer 3 to 5 minutes or until heated through and Mozzarella is melted. Sprinkle with snipped parsley. Serve from Frypan.

STUFFED TEENBURGERS
4 servings

1 package (3 ounces) cream
  cheese
1½ tablespoons dry onion soup
  mix
½ cup fine-chopped parsley
2 pounds ground chuck

Mix softened cream cheese, soup mix and parsley. On a wet board, flatten chuck to 6- by 12-inch rectangle with a wet knife and cut into 8 equal parts. Divide cream cheese mixture over four of these parts, spreading to within ¼ inch of the edges. Top with remaining four pieces of meat. Press edges together, sealing with damp fingers. Heat Multi-Cooker Frypan to 350°. Grease lightly. Cook burgers until brown on each side, turning carefully.

Serving style: Take your Multi-Cooker Frypan to the family room, dining room or wherever teens are gathered, and cook on the spot—doubling or tripling the recipe as necessary.

Other delicious fillings: Half slices of crisp bacon on thick slice of avocado; chopped pickled beets, onion and capers bound with raw egg yolk; mashed hard-cooked egg, grated cheese and mustard; blue cheese, minced radishes and onions, bound with sour cream; slice of tomato topped with strips of Cheddar cheese.

SHRIMP BAHAMA
6 to 8 servings

2 pounds peeled, deveined
  shrimp
¼ cup olive oil
¼ cup butter
½ cup brandy
1 teaspoon flour
½ cup cream
½ cup fish stock or clam juice
2 tablespoons curry powder

4 slices fresh pineapple, cut into
large pieces
3 bananas, cut into ½-inch
slices

Marinate the raw shrimp in the
oil for 3 hours. Preheat Multi-
Cooker Frypan to 325°. Melt
butter in Frypan; sauté shrimp
2 to 3 minutes. Add brandy and
light with a match. Let flames
die down. Sprinkle with flour
and stir to blend. Add remaining
ingredients; turn Frypan down
to Simmer and cook 10 minutes.

Serving style: With this delicious
and unusual curry serve hot
parslied rice, a salad of mixed
greens with croutons and cubes
of mild cheese. Because it takes
so short a time, and because the
ingredients are so attractive, this
is a good cook-at-table dish.

CHEESED CORNED BEEF HASH
4 servings

2 tablespoons fat
1 onion, chopped
1 green pepper, chopped
1 can (1 pound) corned beef
hash
½ pound sharp Cheddar cheese,
diced

Melt fat in Multi-Cooker Frypan set at 300°. Sauté onion and
pepper 5 minutes. Add hash and
cook until lightly browned, stirring often. Stir in Cheddar and
cook just long enough to melt
it partially.

FRENCH FRIED SHRIMP
4 servings

2 pounds cooked, deveined
shrimp
Lemon juice
Salt, pepper
Celery salt
Flour
2 eggs
½ cup milk or water
Fine dry bread crumbs
Shortening

Dip shrimp into lemon juice,
sprinkle lightly with salt, pepper
and celery salt. Roll in flour.
Beat eggs slightly; stir in milk.
Dip shrimp into mixture, then
into crumbs. Remove excess.
Fry in preheated shortening at
375° in Sunbeam Cooker and
Deep Fryer until golden brown,
about 2 minutes. Drain. Put on
paper towels. Serve with cocktail
sauce, ketchup, or chili sauce.

FRENCH-TOASTED HAMWICHES
4 servings

8 slices firm-type bread
Softened butter or margarine
Prepared mustard
4 slices cooked ham
8 slices cooked chicken
2 eggs
⅔ cup milk
¼ teaspoon salt

Spread bread with softened but-

Recipe books for new Blenders and Mixers
contain information on speed settings for
other models in front, Instruction Section.   119

ter, then with a little mustard. Place ham on 4 bread slices, topping each ham slice with 2 chicken slices. Top with remaining bread. Heat Multi-Cooker Frypan to 340°. Melt 1 tablespoon butter in Frypan. Combine eggs, milk and salt. Beat with Mixmaster Hand Mixer until blended. Dip both sides of sandwiches into egg mixture; sauté in melted butter until well browned on both sides.

Serving style: These, with potato chips, bread-and-butter pickles and Mint Malt (page 81) make a satisfying Saturday lunch.

PARTY CRAB MEAT
6 servings

3 tablespoons butter
4 large mushrooms, sliced
2 teaspoons finely chopped shallots
2 tablespoons tomato paste
1¼ cups heavy cream, divided
1 pound fresh, canned or frozen lump crab meat, picked over but not broken up
Salt, pepper
2 egg yolks
1 teaspoon snipped parsley
1 teaspoon snipped chives
Pinch tarragon
¼ cup brandy
Hot cooked rice

Assemble ingredients. At table: Melt butter in a Multi-Cooker Frypan at 280°. Add mushrooms and cook about 5 min-

utes, stirring. Add shallots and cook until liquid from mushrooms has disappeared. Stir in tomato paste and blend thoroughly. Stir in 1 cup cream and cook, stirring constantly until mixture begins to simmer and is well blended. Turn Frypan to Simmer. Add crab meat. Season to taste with salt and pepper. Stir gently and heat well. Beat together egg yolks and ¼ cup cream. Stir egg mixture slowly into crab meat. Add parsley, chives and tarragon. Heat, stirring constantly until mixture is hot. *Do not boil.* Stir in brandy. Serve immediately over hot cooked rice.

SAUTEED CARROTS
4 servings

8 carrots
¼ teaspoon salt
Sugar
¼ cup butter or margarine

Scrape carrots and cut in half lengthwise. Cook until almost tender in small amount of boiling salted water. Drain on rack. Dip in granulated sugar. Preheat Multi-Cooker Frypan to 300°; add butter. Melt, add carrots; sauté to golden color, turning frequently.

COOKING WITH A FOREIGN FLAVOR

How about dinner in Greece? Brunch in Mexico? Luncheon in Australia? Want to sample the foods of France, of Hungary, of Holland, of many other countries? Here are recipes to take you on a cook's tour of the world without ever leaving your own kitchen. Browse here for new ideas to add zest to many kinds of meals, with your Sunbeam Appliances to help you.

POACHED FISH WITH GARLIC SAUCE
6 to 8 servings

4 cloves garlic, crushed
1 teaspoon salt
1 teaspoon dry mustard
¼ teaspoon pepper
3 egg yolks
¼ cup lemon juice
1½ cups olive oil (or salad oil)
1 bottle (8 ounces) clam juice
1 cup white wine
½ cup sliced scallions
1 bay leaf
1 teaspoon tarragon
½ teaspoon salt
2 pounds cod fillets
2 packages (10 ounces each) frozen broccoli spears
3 egg yolks

Place first 6 ingredients into Sunbeam Blender. Process at Whip, 30 seconds. Turn Blender to Mix, and pour oil in gradually, as if making mayonnaise. Chill this sauce. Combine clam juice, wine, scallions, bay leaf, tarragon and ½ teaspoon salt in Multi-Cooker Frypan. Turn dial to 300° and bring to a boil. Reduce heat to Simmer and add fillets. Cover and cook gently 15 to 20 minutes or until fish flakes. Remove fish from liquid and drain; keep warm on serving platter. Remove bay leaf from liquid; bring liquid in Multi-Cooker Frypan to a boil at 300°. Add broccoli, breaking apart with a fork. When liquid boils again, turn heat down to Simmer, cover and cook broccoli 8 to 10 minutes. Drain, reserving liquid. Place broccoli around fish on platter. Keep warm. In Blender place 1 cup of chilled sauce, 3 egg yolks and ¼ cup of liquid in which fish and broccoli were cooked. Blend 1 minute at Cream. Add to liquid in Multi-Cooker Frypan; heat at Simmer until thickened. *Do not boil.* Pour over fish and broccoli. Serve remaining chilled sauce with this dish.

Good to know: In Provence, the

Recipe books for new Blenders and Mixers contain information on speed settings for other models in front, Instruction Section.

121

home of this delicious fish dish, the delicacy is called Morue à l'Aioli—aioli is the chilled garlic sauce. Try it with other fish.

FILLET OF SOLE WERNER
4 servings

⅓ cup butter or margarine
1 box (8 ounces) frozen
    artichoke hearts
½ pound mushrooms, sliced
1½ pounds fillet of sole, cut
    into strips
4 tomatoes peeled, seeded,
    minced
¾ cup white wine
1 cup clam juice
1 tablespoon butter or
    margarine
1 tablespoon flour
¾ cup Hollandaise Sauce
    (page 97)
⅓ cup heavy cream, whipped
1 tablespoon lemon juice
4 patty shells
4 truffles (optional)

Melt butter in Multi-Cooker Frypan with Dial set at 325°. Sauté artichokes in butter 5 minutes. Add mushrooms; sauté 2 minutes. Add fish, tomatoes, wine and clam juice. Bring to a boil; turn Dial to Simmer. Cook 8 to 10 minutes or until fish flakes. Remove fish and vegetables from Frypan. Combine butter and flour; stir into liquid in Frypan. Cook until thickened, 2 or 3 minutes. Turn off heat and let mixture cool about 5 minutes. Fold Hollandaise and whipped cream into mixture. Add lemon juice. Taste and correct seasoning. Turn Frypan Dial to Simmer. Return fish and vegetables to sauce. Cook just until heated through—*do not boil.* Spoon into patty shells, garnish with truffles.

Good to know: This delicious German way with sole is worth every moment of the time it takes. Use patty shells from the bakery, or bake the good frozen ones. If you don't want to use truffles, garnish with black olive.

BOEUF BOURGUIGNONNE
6 servings

2½ pounds beef chuck or
round, cut into 1½-inch pieces
1½ teaspoons salt
¼ teaspoon pepper
¼ pound salt pork
1 medium onion, coarsely
    chopped
1 small clove garlic, minced
1½ cups dry red wine
1 small bay leaf
2 tablespoons chopped parsley
½ teaspoon thyme
½ pound fresh mushrooms,
    sliced
1½ tablespoons flour

Sprinkle beef with salt and pepper. Cut salt pork into small cubes. Set Dial of Sunbeam Cooker and Deep Fryer at 300°. When hot, add salt pork pieces and cook until golden brown. Remove salt pork. Add beef cubes to hot fat, a few pieces at a time. Brown well on all sides and remove. Add onion to fat and cook until onion is just tender. Return salt pork and beef to cooker. Add garlic, wine, bay leaf, parsley and thyme. Reduce heat to Simmer. Cover and simmer about 2 hours or until meat is tender. Add additional wine if necessary during cooking time. Add mushrooms during the last 15 minutes of the cooking time. Remove bay leaf. Combine flour with a little cold water to make a smooth paste. Stir into hot mixture, and cook, stirring until mixture is smooth and slightly thickened.

CLASSIC BEEF ROLLS
6 servings

½ pound bulk pork sausage
6 cooked ham slices, ¼ inch
thick
6 rare roast beef slices, ¼ inch
thick
2 tablespoons cooking oil
2 cups sliced onions
2 cups sliced carrots
1 cup red wine
1 can (10½ ounces) beef broth
2 tablespoons flour

In Multi-Cooker Frypan set at 325°, brown sausage meat,

breaking it up with a fork into small pieces. Turn off Frypan. Remove sausage and drain off liquid. Cool sausage slightly and divide into 6 portions. Place 1 ham slice on each beef slice and place 1 portion of sausage in center of ham slice. Roll like a jelly roll and secure with toothpicks. Heat cooking oil in Multi-Cooker Frypan set at 325°. Sauté onions and carrots in oil until tender, about 10 minutes. Add wine and beef broth. Place meat rolls on top of vegetables. Reduce heat to Simmer; cover and simmer 10 minutes. Remove meat to serving dish and keep warm. Blend flour smooth in ¼ cup water. Add to Frypan. Turn Dial up to 325° and bring to a boil, stirring constantly. Pour vegetable sauce over meat rolls.

Good to know: In France, their home, these are Roulades de Boeuf. Serve them with crusty bread, a hearty green salad.

ROLLED FLANK STEAK
6 servings

5 eggs
⅓ cup grated Cheddar cheese
2 tablespoons butter or
margarine
3-pound flank steak
½ teaspoon salt
½ teaspoon pepper
1 small pimiento, diced
½ cup cooked green peas
6 cups beef broth

Using Mixmaster Hand Mixer, set at medium speed, beat eggs and Cheddar together. Preheat Multi-Cooker Frypan to 300°. Melt butter, add egg mixture and cook, stirring constantly until eggs are dry. Remove from Frypan. Sprinkle flank steak with salt and pepper. Cover with cooked eggs, pimiento and peas. Roll from the short side and sew. Wrap in cheesecloth and sew again. Place in Sunbeam Cooker and Deep Fryer and add broth. Turn Dial to 300° and bring to a boil. Skim if necessary. Turn Cooker Dial to Simmer. Cover and cook 1½ to 2 hours or until tender. Remove steak from stock; press with a heavy object and refrigerate. Serve cold, cut into slices.

Good to know: Fiambre, as this is known in its native Montevideo, is usually served with an assortment of vegetables marinated in a vinaigrette sauce.

GREEK MACARONI BAKE
8 servings

1 pound ziti macaroni
4 tablespoons butter
2 pounds ground beef
4 tablespoons tomato paste
1 large onion, chopped
4 cloves garlic, finely chopped
Salt, pepper
½ pound Romano cheese, grated
Custard Topping

Cook ziti according to package directions; drain and reserve. Preheat Multi-Cooker Frypan to 340°. Melt butter in Frypan and cook beef, stirring until brown. Dilute tomato paste with ½ cup water; add to meat with onion, garlic and salt and pepper to taste. Mix well. Turn Frypan Dial to Simmer and cook until liquid is absorbed. Grease a deep 9- by 11-inch baking dish. Arrange alternate layers of macaroni and beef, sprinkling each layer with Romano, reserving ½ cup cheese. Pour half of Custard Topping over casserole. Bake in a preheated 400° F. oven 10 minutes. Pour remaining Custard Topping over casserole, sprinkle with reserved cheese. Bake 5 minutes, then lower heat to 325° F. and bake 40 minutes longer or until well browned. Cut into sections, serve hot.

CUSTARD TOPPING

½ cup butter
3 cups milk
3 tablespoons cornstarch
6 eggs

Melt butter in saucepan over low heat. And milk, cook to simmering. Dissolve cornstarch in ½ cup water and add. Cook, stirring until thickened. Cool slightly. Place eggs in large bowl of Mixmaster Mixer. With Dial set at No. 4, beat eggs until well blended. Gradually add milk mixture to eggs, beating constantly.

Good to know: This great Greek "everyday" dish is known at home as Pastitsio.

MANDARIN BEEF
4 to 6 servings

2 tablespoons olive oil
2 pounds flank steak, cut across grain into thin strips
¼ teaspoon garlic powder
½ teaspoon salt
⅛ teaspoon pepper
¼ teaspoon ground ginger
¼ cup soy sauce
½ teaspoon sugar
2 tomatoes, quartered
2 green peppers, cut into chunks
1 can bean sprouts, drained
1 tablespoon cornstarch

Heat Multi-Cooker Frypan to 380°. Place oil in Frypan and add beef, garlic powder, salt, pepper and ginger. Brown beef quickly. Turn Frypan to Simmer. Add soy sauce and sugar. Cook, covered, 5 minutes. Add tomatoes, pepper and bean sprouts. Bring to a boil, cover and cook 5 minutes. Combine cornstarch and ¼ cup water; add to beef mixture. Cook, stirring until slightly thickened.
Serving style: This Chinese dish calls for fluffy white rice. Serve preserved kumquats for dessert.

VEAL IN CREAM
4 servings

2 pounds veal steak, ½ inch thick
1 teaspoon salt
¼ teaspoon white pepper
3 tablespoons butter or margarine
¼ cup dry white wine
1½ cups heavy cream
2 tablespoons brandy

Using Sunbeam Knife, cut veal into large julienne strips. Dry thoroughly, season with salt and pepper. Heat Multi-Cooker Frypan to 350°. Add 2 tablespoons butter. When butter has foamed and foam starts to subside, add veal. Sauté about 8 minutes, browning well on all sides. Remove meat and keep it warm. Add wine to Frypan and cook until liquid is reduced to about ¼ cup. Add cream, turn heat down to Simmer. Cook 5 minutes until cream has reduced and thickened slightly. Taste, correct seasoning. Add meat, remaining butter and brandy. Mix well; simmer 2 minutes or until meat is heated through. Serve at once.

Good to know: This Emincé de Veau—homeland Switzerland— is delicious served on toast. And, unlike many foreign recipes, it's quick-and-easy to make.

Recipe books for new Blenders and Mixers contain information on speed settings for other models in front, Instruction Section.

125

SUKIYAKI
4 to 6 servings

1 cup soy sauce
1 cup water
½ cup sake (rice wine) or
dry white wine
3 tablespoons sugar
2 pounds sirloin or eye of rib,
sliced ⅛ inch thin
Suet
1 small can yam noodles or dried
cellophane noodles, soaked
1 small can bamboo shoots
4 bunches scallions, cut into
1½-inch lengths
2 large onions, thinly sliced
Optional vegetables:
Fresh mushrooms
Celery
Spinach
Watercress
Bean sprouts
Chinese cabbage
Snow peas
Bean curd cubes

Combine soy sauce, water, sake and sugar in a pitcher and set aside. Arrange meat on 1 large or 2 medium-sized trays or platters. Cut suet into 3 or 4 pieces and place on top of meat. Arrange prepared vegetables attractively around meat on platters. Drain noodles and bamboo shoots and place around meat. Arrange scallions and onions on platter. Select 2 or 3 vegetables from list to go on platter. Mushrooms should be thinly sliced.

Celery should be cleaned and cut at a diagonal. Spinach should be small center leaves. Chinese cabbage should be cut into shreds. Remove tips and strings from snow peas. Prepare Sukiyaki at table in 2 separate cookings. Preheat Sunbeam Multi-Cooker Frypan at 380° F. Rub bottom of hot Frypan with suet. Add half of the meat; stir-fry 1 minute. Add half of the noodles, bamboo shoots, scallions, onions and selected vegetables. Pour half of the sauce mixture over top. Cook, uncovered, about 7 minutes or until crisply tender, stirring lightly. Serve immediately. Continue with remaining meat and vegetables.

ITALIAN EGGPLANT PARMIGIANA
4 servings

1 medium eggplant, peeled, cut
into ¼-inch slices
½ cup flour
Salt, pepper
1 egg
1 tablespoon milk
¼ cup olive oil
2 cups Italian Tomato Sauce
½ cup grated Parmesan cheese
½ pound Mozzarella cheese,
sliced

Salt eggplant slices and let stand 1 hour. Rinse, pat dry. Season flour with salt and pepper; dredge eggplant slices. Mix egg and milk. Heat Multi-Cooker

Frypan to 360°. Put olive oil into Frypan and heat. Dip eggplant slices into egg-milk mixture. Sauté 3 to 4 minutes on each side. Reserve. Put a few tablespoons Italian Tomato Sauce into the bottom of a shallow casserole. Cover with a layer of eggplant slices. Sprinkle with part of the Parmesan. Spread on more Tomato Sauce. Top with Mozzarella slices. Repeat. Bake in a preheated 350° F. oven 30 minutes.

ITALIAN TOMATO SAUCE
5 to 6 cups

1 can (28 ounces) Italian plum
tomatoes
4 tablespoons olive oil
3 large onions, chopped
3 cloves garlic, finely chopped
2 cans (6 ounces each) tomato
paste
1½ teaspoons basil
1 teaspoon oregano
1 teaspoon sugar
1 teaspoon salt
½ teaspoon black pepper

Place tomatoes, half at a time, into Sunbeam Blender and process at Puree 1 minute. In Sunbeam Cooker and Deep Fryer, heat olive oil to 360°. Sauté onions and garlic in olive oil until soft but not brown. Add tomato purée and remaining ingredients. Turn Dial to first M in Simmer. Cook sauce, uncovered, two hours, stirring occasionally. If necessary, add a little water as the sauce cooks.

POORI
8 to 10 pieces

2 cups all-purpose flour
1 teaspoon salt
¼ pound butter or margarine
Vegetable shortening or oil for
deep frying

Sift flour and salt into a bowl. Using two knives or a pastry cutter, cut in the butter until small particles form. Stir in water enough to make a soft dough. Place the dough on a lightly floured board and knead until it is smooth and holds together. Roll out dough as thin as possible with a lightly floured rolling pin. Cut into 5-inch circles. Heat the oil or vegetable shortening in Sunbeam Cooker and Deep Fryer to 370°. Fry each circle of dough 2 to 3 minutes, turning once until lightly browned. Serve hot.

Good to know: This is Indian bread and makes a wonderful addition to a curry meal. If you are entertaining, prepare the dough in advance and refrigerate the circles, separated by sheets of wax paper or foil until ready to use. Bring your Sunbeam Cooker and Deep Fryer to the table and cook the Poori "to order" for each guest.

COQ AU VIN
8 servings

4 slices bacon
½ cup butter or margarine
2 broiler-fryers cut into quarters
16 small white onions, peeled,
whole
16 large whole mushrooms
2 cloves garlic, minced
1 bunch scallions, cleaned and
cut up
¼ cup flour
3 cups dry red table wine
2 chicken bouillon cubes
2 teaspoons salt
¼ teaspoon pepper
½ teaspoon thyme
1 bay leaf

Preheat Sunbeam Cooker and Deep Fryer to 300°. Cut bacon into small pieces. Cook bacon until crisp. Remove bacon pieces from Cooker and reserve. Add butter to bacon fat. Brown chicken pieces well on all sides in hot fat. Remove chicken and reserve. Place whole onions and mushrooms in Cooker and brown lightly. Remove onions and mushrooms. Pour drippings out of Cooker, reserving 2 tablespoonfuls. Return reserved drippings to Cooker. Add garlic and scallions and cook at 300° until scallions are limp. Stir in flour and cook 2 minutes, stirring constantly until flour is browned. Turn off heat and stir in wine, bouillon cubes and 1 cup boiling water. Turn dial to 300° and cook, stirring until mixture comes to a boil. Season with salt, pepper, thyme and bay leaf. Add bacon bits, chicken pieces, onions and mushrooms. Cover tightly, turn heat to Simmer and cook 30 to 45 minutes or until chicken is tender. Remove bay leaf before serving.

ITALIAN CHEESECAKE
6 servings

½ package (10 ounces) pie
crust mix
1 pound ricotta cheese
7 eggs
1 cup sugar
1 teaspoon grated orange rind
1 teaspoon grated lemon rind
3 tablespoons diced mixed
candied fruit
2 teaspoons vanilla
1 teaspoon salt

Preheat oven to 350° F. Prepare pastry according to package directions. Roll to about an 11-inch circle. Fit loosely into a lightly greased and floured 9-inch cake pan with straight sides. Prick with a fork. Place ricotta in large bowl of Mixmaster Mixer. Add eggs and sugar. Beat at No. 2 until thoroughly blended. Turn to No. 1 and blend in remaining ingredients. Pour into pastry shell and bake 1½ hours or until a knife inserted in center comes out clean. Serve warm or cold.

*Recipe books for new Blenders and Mixers
contain information on speed settings for
other models in front, Instruction Section.*

129

COLD WINE CUSTARD
6 servings

6 egg yolks
6 tablespoons sugar
½ cup sweet Marsala wine
1 cup heavy cream
Maraschino cherries

Put egg yolks into small Mixmaster Mixer bowl. With Dial at No. 2, beat yolks until blended. Continue beating and add the sugar, a tablespoon at a time. Continuing to beat, add wine gradually. Place mixture in top of a double boiler. Cook over boiling water, stirring constantly until thickened, 3 to 4 minutes. Cool. Place cream in large Mixmaster Mixer bowl. With Dial set at No. 9, whip cream stiff. With Dial set at No. 1, fold in cooled custard. Spoon into serving dishes, top each with a maraschino cherry and refrigerate.

Good to know: This is the cold version of Italy's famous and delicious Zabaglione.

GREEK NUT CAKE
about 20 servings

8 slices zwieback
Almonds
Walnuts
Rind of 1 orange
6 eggs, separated
¾ cup sugar
½ teaspoon vanilla

1 cup sugar
1-inch piece stick cinnamon
1 slice lemon
¼ cup light rum

Preheat oven to 350° F. Butter 9½- by 13- by 2-inch baking pan. Break each slice of zwieback into three pieces. Put several pieces at a time into Sunbeam Blender. Cover and process at Grate until crumbed. Repeat until all zwieback is used; reserve. With Blender set at Grate, finely grate sufficient almonds, then walnuts, to make 1½ cups of each. Reserve. Place orange rind, cut into pieces, in Blender. With Blender set at Grate, process until finely grated. Reserve. Place egg whites in large bowl. Beat with Mixmaster Hand Mixer at highest speed until stiff but not dry. Reserve. In large Mixmaster Mixer bowl combine egg yolks, ¾ cup sugar and vanilla. Beat at No. 6 until thick and pale yellow. With Dial set at No. 1, fold in egg whites. Combine crumbs, nuts and orange rind; fold into mixture. Pour batter into well-buttered 9½- by 13- by 2-inch baking pan. Bake 45 minutes. In a saucepan, over low heat, dissolve 1 cup sugar in 2 cups water with stick cinnamon and lemon slice. Remove from heat and stir in rum. As soon as cake is removed from oven, strain this hot syrup over cake. Cool in pan.

 or

IRANIAN PANCAKES
6 servings

2 eggs, separated
1 cup plain yogurt
¾ cup flour
1 tablespoon sugar
1 teaspoon baking soda
½ teaspoon salt
½ cup butter or margarine,
melted

In small bowl of Mixmaster Mixer beat egg whites at No. 12 until stiff but not dry. Reserve. In large bowl of Mixmaster Mixer combine yogurt and egg yolks. Beat at No. 2 until blended. Sift together flour, sugar, soda and salt. Add to yogurt mixture, beating at No. 2 until blended. Add melted butter. Turn Mixmaster Mixer Dial to No. 1 and fold in egg whites. Preheat Sunbeam Griddle or Multi-Cooker Frypan to 380°. Bake by tablespoonfuls until lightly browned on both sides, turning only once.

Serving style: Serve the Iranian way with honey heated with rose water or lime juice.

GOLDEN CLOUDS
6 servings, 3 clouds per serving

12 egg yolks
1 egg white
2 cups sugar
1 teaspoon vanilla

Preheat oven to 325° F. With Mixmaster Mixer set at No. 8, beat egg yolks and egg white together until thick and lemon-colored, about 20 minutes. Lightly butter small custard cups. Pour 2 tablespoons of egg mixture into each custard cup. Set cups in a pan of hot water. Bake 30 minutes. While Clouds are baking, combine sugar and 3½ cups water in a saucepan. Bring to a boil and simmer 5 minutes. Add vanilla, remove from heat. When Clouds are baked, drop each into this warm syrup and turn to coat; place on a shallow dish and chill. Chill remaining syrup. Serve Clouds with a little syrup over each serving.

Good to know: In Brazil, where these are called Papos de Anjo, they are served at sidewalk cafés with tiny cups of very hot, very black coffee.

Other ways: Use hot maple syrup instead of the vanilla syrup; top with chopped pecans . . . top with lemon hard sauce and a dollop of whipped cream . . . top with custard and toasted coconut.

DELECTABLE DESSERTS

Every meal should have a happy ending. Here are many sweets, from simple ones to elaborate, to give that final, delicious touch to any meal you serve. Your Sunbeam Blender and Mixmaster Mixer are your helpers here—they make whipping up wonderful desserts so easy you'll be making cakes, pies and cookies, hot treats and cold, every day of the week.

CHOCOLATE-NUT TORTE
10 servings

2 cups sifted cake flour
1½ cups sugar
1 teaspoon salt
1 teaspoon baking soda
1 cup sour cream
⅓ cup butter or margarine,
softened
2 eggs
1 teaspoon almond extract
3 squares (1 ounce each)
unsweetened chocolate, melted
Nut Filling
Fluffy Frosting (page 141)

Preheat oven to 350° F. Into large Mixmaster Mixer bowl sift flour, sugar, salt and baking soda. Add sour cream and butter. With Dial set at No. 2, blend ingredients; then beat at No. 5 until well blended. Beat in 1 egg, then the other. Add almond extract, melted chocolate and ¼ cup hot water. Beat until well blended. Line 2 round 8-inch cake pans with wax paper; grease and lightly flour the paper. Divide batter between pans. Bake 35 minutes or until cake tester inserted in center comes out clean. Cool on rack 5 minutes. Remove cake from pans; peel off paper and complete cooling. Split each layer crosswise to make a total of 4 layers. Spread Nut Filling between layers. Top with Fluffy Frosting.

NUT FILLING

¾ cup sugar
¾ cup evaporated milk
3 egg yolks
½ cup butter or margarine
1 teaspoon vanilla
1 can (3½ ounces) flaked
coconut
1 cup fine-chopped walnuts

In a saucepan over medium-high heat, cook sugar, milk, egg yolks, butter and vanilla, stirring constantly until thickened. Remove from heat. Mix in coconut and nuts thoroughly. Cool.

Recipe books for new Blenders and Mixers
contain information on speed settings for
other models in front, Instruction Section.

133

DRESSED-UP CAKE MIXES

Using a box of cake mix, a couple of extra ingredients and a little ingenuity, you can turn out fine-textured, pound-cake-type cakes of many kinds. They are family-sized and have better keeping qualities than the ordinary make-from-a-mix cake. For all of them, the method is the same—and very simple. Turn the ingredients into the large Mixmaster Mixer bowl; blend 1 minute at No. 2; turn the dial to No. 6 and beat 2 minutes. Bake in a greased tube pan or Bundt mold, in a preheated 350° F. oven, 45 to 55 minutes or until the cake tests done with a toothpick. Let stand in the pan about 5 minutes, then turn out to cool. These cakes can be served plain, frosted or glazed, as you like, or sprinkled with confectioners' sugar. Each of these recipes makes 1 10-inch cake.

ORANGE-PLUS CAKE

1 package white cake mix
4 eggs
½ cup cooking oil
1 cup fresh or reconstituted frozen orange juice
1 package vanilla or lemon instant pudding mix

1 tablespoon grated orange rind
½ teaspoon ground mace

Mix and bake as above.

LEMON CAKE

1 package yellow cake mix
4 eggs
½ cup cooking oil
1 cup water
1 package lemon instant pudding mix
1 teaspoon lemon extract or
1 tablespoon grated lemon rind

Mix and bake as above.

MOCHA BUNDT CAKE

1 package chocolate or devil's food cake mix
4 eggs
½ cup cooking oil
1 cup water
1 package chocolate instant pudding mix
1 tablespoon dry instant coffee
1 teaspoon vanilla

Mix and bake as above—in a Bundt pan if desired.

SILVER LAYER CAKE
10 to 12 servings

2½ cups sifted cake flour
1½ cups granulated sugar
3 teaspoons baking powder
1 teaspoon salt
½ cup soft shortening
1¼ cups milk, divided

Recipe books for new Blenders and Mixers contain information on speed settings for other models in front, Instruction Section.

135

1½ teaspoons vanilla
¼ teaspoon almond extract
3 egg whites

Preheat oven to 350° F. Grease, then line with wax paper, 2 8-inch layer pans 1½ inches deep. Sift into large Mixmaster Mixer bowl sifted flour, sugar, baking powder and salt. Add shortening, ¾ cup milk and flavorings. Beat 30 seconds at No. 1 to moisten flour, then 2 minutes at No. 4. Add remaining milk and the egg whites; beat 1½ minutes longer. Divide evenly into pans. Bake about 30 minutes. Cool.

Birthday Cake: Fill with lemon filling, ice with Fluffy Frosting (page 141), sprinkle thickly with moist coconut. Also may be baked in tier cake pans, iced with Fluffy Frosting and decorated with artificial blossoms and candles. Write Happy Birthday on the top with tinted confectioners sugar icing.

Chocolate Fleck Cake: Fold into batter ½ cup grated or finely shredded sweet baking chocolate as final step.

Cherry Cake: Drain 4-ounce bottle of maraschino cherries, chop finely, lay on paper towels, press with another piece of towel to absorb juice. Pour ⅓ of cake batter into greased 9-inch layer pans. Sprinkle part of cherries on batter. Add more batter and sprinkle cherries on top. Bake, cool, ice; sprinkle with coconut, garnish with cherries.

Chocolate Marble Cake: Melt 1 square chocolate. Blend in 1 tablespoon sugar, ¼ teaspoon soda, 2 tablespoons water. Beat into ⅓ of batter only until blended. Alternate spoonfuls of white and chocolate batter in pans. Cut through batter with a knife 3 times. Bake.

JIFFY ONE-EGG CAKE
9 servings

1½ cups sifted cake flour
¾ cup granulated sugar
2 teaspoons baking powder
½ teaspoon salt
⅓ cup soft shortening
½ cup milk
1 teaspoon vanilla or
1 tablespoon grated orange or
lemon rind
1 egg

Preheat oven to 375° F. Grease, then dust with flour, 8-inch-square pan. Sift into large bowl of Mixmaster Mixer sifted flour, sugar, baking powder and salt. Add shortening, milk and flavoring. Beat at No. 1 30 seconds, then at No. 4 2 minutes; add egg, beat 1 minute longer. Turn into pan. Bake about 25 minutes or until done. Cool and ice as desired.

Cupcakes: Fill greased cupcake pans only ½ full of batter. Bake 15 to 20 minutes until done. Ice or use as individual shortcakes.

Coffee Cake with Streusel Topping: Mix 2 tablespoons soft butter, ½ cup brown sugar, firmly packed, 1 teaspoon cinnamon, 2 tablespoons flour and ⅓ cup chopped nuts. Pour batter into greased 8- by 8- by 2-inch pan. Sprinkle with topping. Bake as directed.

Upside-Down Cake: Melt 2 tablespoons butter or margarine in bottom of 8- or 9-inch-square pan; remove from heat. Sprinkle with ½ cup brown sugar, packed. Arrange drained canned fruit such as pineapple slices, peach halves or fruit cocktail over sugar. Garnish with maraschino cherries and nuts, if desired. Pour batter over fruit. Bake at 350° F. about 45 minutes or until done. Cool in pan on wire rack 10 minutes, then run spatula around edges and invert on serving plate. Serve warm with whipped cream cheese, cream or ice cream.

LARGE BIRTHDAY CAKE
12 to 14 servings

3 cups sifted cake flour
3 teaspoons baking powder
¾ teaspoon salt
1 cup soft butter
or margarine
2 cups granulated sugar
4 eggs
1 cup milk
2 teaspoons vanilla

Preheat oven to 375° F. Grease, then line 3 9-inch layer pans with wax paper. Sift together twice the sifted flour, baking

powder and salt. In large bowl of Mixmaster Mixer, cream butter and sugar at No. 7 2½ minutes. Add eggs, one at a time, beating 30 seconds at No. 7 after each addition. At No. 3, beat in alternately, about 30 seconds each time, flour mixture in 4 additions and milk combined with flavoring in 3 additions, starting and ending with flour mixture. Beat 1 minute after last addition. Turn into pans. Bake about 25 to 30 minutes. Cool.

CHOCOLATE FUDGE CAKE
10 to 12 servings

2¼ cups sifted cake flour
1 cup sugar
1 teaspoon salt
1½ teaspoons baking soda
1 cup brown sugar, packed
½ cup soft shortening
3 squares unsweetened
chocolate, melted
1¼ cups milk, buttermilk or
sour milk, divided
1½ teaspoons vanilla
3 eggs

Preheat oven to 350° F. Grease, then line with wax paper, 2 9-inch layer pans. Sift into large Mixmaster Mixer bowl sifted flour, granulated sugar, salt and soda. Add brown sugar, shortening, chocolate, ¾ cup milk and vanilla. Beat 30 seconds at No. 1 to moisten flour, then 2 minutes at No. 4. Add remain-

Recipe books for new Blenders and Mixers
contain information on speed settings for
other models in front, Instruction Section.

137

ing milk and eggs. Beat 1½ minutes longer. Pour into pans. Bake 35 to 40 minutes. Cool.

ANGEL FOOD CAKE
12 servings

1¼ cups egg whites
1 cup plus 2 tablespoons sifted
cake flour
1½ cups sugar, divided
½ teaspoon salt
1¼ teaspoons cream of tartar
1 teaspoon vanilla extract
¼ teaspoon almond extract

Let egg whites stand at room temperature about 1 hour. Preheat oven to 375° F. Sift together flour and 1 cup of the sugar 4 times. Reserve. In large bowl of Mixmaster Mixer combine egg whites and remaining ingredients. Beat at highest speed until egg whites are stiff and form soft peaks, 1½ to 2 minutes. Do not overbeat. Turn speed to No. 6 and beat while gradually adding remaining sugar. Beat until sugar is just blended. Turn speed to No. 1. Sprinkle in sifted flour mixture evenly and quickly, scraping up and over with a folding motion, only until blended, about 1½ minutes. Remove bowl from Mixer and cut through batter, folding over and over a few times with a rubber scraper. Carefully spoon batter into an ungreased 10-inch tube pan. Cut through batter with a spatula,

going around in widening circles 6 times without lifting spatula. Bake 30 to 35 minutes or until a cake tester inserted comes out clean. Remove from oven and invert at once; let *hang* upside down until completely cold. Then insert spatula between cake and side of pan, moving it around and lifting it to loosen cake. Loosen around tube, invert on plate, loosen bottom and lift pan off.

PECAN LOG
12 servings

5 ounces (about) shelled pecans
1 teaspoon baking powder
6 eggs, separated
¾ cup sugar
2 cups heavy cream
1 teaspoon vanilla
2 tablespoons sugar

Preheat oven to 350° F. Using Sunbeam Blender set at Chop, process the pecans to make 1½ cups, chopped very fine. Mix in baking powder and reserve. Place the egg yolks in the small Mixmaster Mixer bowl, the whites in the large bowl. Beat the egg whites with Dial set at highest speed until they form stiff peaks. Reserve. Add ¾ cup sugar to yolks and beat at No. 8 until thick and lemon-colored. Turn Dial to No. 1 and fold in pecan mixture. Place large bowl on turntable. With Dial at No. 1 fold yolk mixture into whites.

Recipe books for new Blenders and Mixers
contain information on speed settings for
other models in front, Instruction Section.

Grease a 15½- by 10½- by 1-inch jelly roll pan; cover bottom with wax paper and grease the paper. Pour in batter and spread evenly. Bake 20 to 30 minutes or until cake starts to pull away from sides of pan. Leave cake in pan, cover with a damp towel and refrigerate. About 1 hour before serving, place cream in large Mixmaster Mixer bowl. With Dial set at No. 9, beat cream until stiff. Turn Dial to No. 1 and add vanilla and 2 tablespoons sugar. Turn cake over onto damp towel and remove pan. Peel off paper. Spread whipped cream on cake and roll from long side like a jelly roll. Refrigerate. Slice and serve chilled.

Serving style: This may be served plain, with additional whipped cream, with a thin custard sauce or with crushed and sweetened strawberries.

STRAWBERRY CHEESECAKE
12 servings

*32 slices zwieback
(approximately)
1¼ cups sugar, divided
¾ teaspoon cinnamon
⅓ cup melted butter or
margarine
4 eggs
1 pound cottage cheese*

*¾ pound (1½ 8-ounce
packages or 4 3-ounce packages)
cream cheese
4 tablespoons flour
1 cup light cream
1½ teaspoons grated lemon
rind
1½ teaspoons lemon juice
⅛ teaspoon salt
Strawberry Glaze*

Preheat oven to 350° F. Process zwieback in Sunbeam Blender at Grate to produce 1½ cups fine crumbs. Mix crumbs, ¼ cup sugar, cinnamon and melted butter. Line sides and bottom of a 10-inch spring-form pan with this mixture. Place eggs in large bowl of Mixmaster Mixer. Set Dial at No. 5 and beat well. Beat in remaining sugar, cottage cheese, cream cheese, flour, cream, rind, juice and salt. Pour mixture into crumb-lined pan and bake 1 hour or until center is set. Turn off oven; open door and let cake cool in oven 1 hour. While it cools, prepare Strawberry Glaze.

STRAWBERRY GLAZE

*1 quart strawberries
4 teaspoons cornstarch
½ cup sugar
1 teaspoon butter or margarine
Few drops red food coloring*

Wash and hull the strawberries. In Sunbeam Blender set at

Puree, process enough of the smaller berries to make 1 cup. Reserve larger berries, leaving them whole. In a saucepan, dissolve cornstarch in ½ cup cold water. Add puréed strawberries and sugar. Bring to a boil; boil 2 minutes. Stir in butter and enough food coloring to tint to desired shade. Arrange whole strawberries on top of cheesecake. Spoon Glaze over berries. Refrigerate.

FLUFFY FROSTING
2 egg whites
1½ cups sugar
1½ teaspoons light corn syrup
⅛ teaspoon salt
1 teaspoon vanilla

Combine ingredients, except vanilla, in top of a double boiler. Add ⅓ cup cold water. Beat at No. 3 speed of Mixmaster Hand Mixer or Mixmaster Mixer removed from stand. Then cook over rapidly boiling water, beating constantly at No. 10 until mixture forms peaks when beater is raised, about 7 minutes. Remove from heat. Add vanilla and beat at No. 10 until of spreading consistency, about 2 minutes. Fills and frosts two 8- or 9-inch layers.

Sea Foam Frosting: Use 1½ cups brown sugar, firmly packed, instead of white sugar.

Lady Baltimore Frosting: Into ⅓ of frosting, blend 2 tablespoons chopped drained maraschino cherries, ¼ cup chopped pecans or walnuts, 1 teaspoon grated orange or lemon rind, ¼ cup chopped figs, dates or raisins and ¼ cup shredded coconut. Use as a filling between layers, frost top and sides with plain frosting.

BASIC UNCOOKED BUTTER FROSTING

⅓ cup soft butter or margarine
3 cups sifted confectioners sugar
Dash salt
¼ cup milk or light cream
1½ teaspoons vanilla

Put butter into small Mixmaster Mixer bowl. Cream a few seconds at No. 4. Stop Mixer; add sugar, salt, milk and vanilla. Beat at No. 2 until blended, then at No. 9 until fluffy, about 2 minutes. Add a little more sugar if needed for right spreading consistency. Fills and frosts a 2-layer cake.

Lemon or Orange Frosting: Use lemon or orange juice instead of milk; add 1 teaspoon grated rind.

Maple Frosting: Use maple syrup instead of milk. Omit vanilla. Decorate with walnut halves.

Strawberry Frosting: Omit vanilla, use crushed berries with juice instead of milk.

Mocha Frosting: Use 1 pound

Recipe books for new Blenders and Mixers
contain information on speed settings for
other models in front, Instruction Section.

141

confectioners sugar, sift ½ cup cocoa with it. Use ⅓ cup strong hot coffee instead of milk.

Chocolate Frosting: Make basic recipe, using ½ cup butter, about 1 pound confectioners sugar. Add 3 squares melted unsweetened chocolate or ½ cup cocoa, 2 egg yolks. Beat until smooth.

SWEDISH FATTIGMAN
50 pastries

2 whole eggs
2 egg yolks
¼ cup confectioners sugar
2 teaspoons melted butter
1 tablespoon brandy
1 tablespoon grated lemon rind
1¾ cups sifted flour
Oil for deep frying

Put eggs and yolks in large bowl of Mixmaster Mixer. Set at highest speed and beat until light and fluffy. Add sugar, melted butter, brandy and lemon rind and continue beating. Turn speed to No. 3 and add flour gradually; mix thoroughly. Turn dough out on a lightly floured board and knead lightly. Chill dough. Heat fat in Sunbeam Cooker and Deep Fryer set at 380° until light goes out. Roll dough out on a lightly floured board as thinly as possible. Cut into strips 2 inches long by 1 inch wide. Cut a gash in the center of each strip and pull one corner of the dough *through the gash.* Fry in

hot fat until light brown, turning occasionally. Lift basket to supports and drain. Drain Fattigman on paper towels.

SPRITZ COOKIES
6 dozens

1 cup butter or margarine
⅔ cup sugar
3 egg yolks
1 teaspoon almond or vanilla extract
2½ cups sifted flour

Preheat oven to 400° F. Cream butter thoroughly in Sunbeam Mixmaster Mixer set at No. 7. Add sugar and continue creaming until mixture is light and fluffy. Beat in egg yolks and flavoring. Add 1 cup flour and beat until batter is smooth. Add remaining flour to dough and mix in by hand until mixture is well blended. Chill dough about 30 minutes. Place dough in a cookie press. Hold press upright and force dough onto an ungreased baking sheet into desired shapes. Bake about 8 minutes or until cookies are set but not brown.

QUICK CHOCOLATE CHIP COOKIES
3 dozens

1¼ cups sifted all-purpose flour
½ teaspoon salt
½ cup soft butter or margarine

Recipe books for new Blenders and Mixers contain information on speed settings for other models in front, Instruction Section.

143

½ cup brown sugar, packed
⅓ cup granulated sugar
1 egg
½ teaspoon vanilla
½ teaspoon baking soda
1 cup semisweet chocolate chips
½ cup chopped nuts

Preheat oven to 375° F. Sift together flour and salt. Cream shortening, sugars, egg and vanilla in Mixmaster Mixer at No. 7 2 minutes. Combine soda and 1 tablespoon hot water. Add to batter along with chocolate chips, nuts and sifted mixture. Beat at No. 1 about 1½ minutes. Drop by half teaspoonfuls on greased cookie sheet. Bake about 10 minutes. Cool.

NUT MACAROONS
5 dozens

2 eggs
½ teaspoon salt
1 teaspoon vanilla
1 cup sugar
3 cups finely ground Brazil
nuts, pecans or walnuts

Preheat oven to 325° F. Put eggs, salt and vanilla into large Mixmaster Mixer bowl. Beat at No. 10 2 minutes. Beat in sugar gradually, beating 1 minute. Add nuts, blend in at No. 1. Drop by small teaspoonfuls onto well-greased and floured cookie sheet, pushing batter off spoon with rubber scraper. Bake about 10 minutes. Cool a few seconds, but remove while soft.

OLD-FASHIONED SOFT SUGAR COOKIES
2½ dozens

3¼ cups sifted all-purpose flour
1 teaspoon baking soda
½ teaspoon salt
½ cup soft butter or margarine
1 cup sugar
1 egg
1½ teaspoons vanilla or
1 teaspoon nutmeg
½ cup sour cream
Sugar

Preheat oven to 400° F. Sift together flour, soda and salt. In large Mixmaster Mixer bowl combine butter, sugar, egg and flavoring. Beat at No. 7 2 minutes. Stop Mixer. Add sour cream and then flour mixture gradually while beating at No. 3 speed about 2 minutes. Chill dough. Roll out on lightly floured surface to ¼-inch thickness. Sprinkle with sugar, roll in lightly. Cut with floured cutter. Place on greased cookie sheet. Bake about 12 minutes until golden brown.

BROWNIES
2½ dozens

1 cup sifted cake flour
½ teaspoon baking powder
¼ teaspoon salt
2 squares unsweetened
chocolate

⅓ cup butter or margarine
1 cup sugar
2 eggs
1 teaspoon vanilla
½ to ¾ cup chopped pecans

Preheat oven to 350° F. Sift together flour, baking powder and salt. Melt chocolate and butter over hot water. Put sugar, eggs and vanilla into large Mixmaster Mixer bowl. Beat at No. 7 2 minutes. Stop Mixer, add chocolate and flour mixture. Beat at No. 1 until blended, then at No. 4 1 minute. Turn into greased 9- by 9- by 2-inch pan. Sprinkle nuts over top. Bake 25 minutes or until done. Cool in pan. When cold, cut into squares.

Good to know: Nuts may be added to batter. If desired, frost brownies as follows: Combine in small Mixmaster Mixer bowl 2 tablespoons soft butter, 1½ cups sifted confectioners sugar, 3 tablespoons water, 2 teaspoons corn syrup, 1 teaspoon vanilla, 2 squares unsweetened chocolate, melted. Beat at No. 3 until blended. Spread on cooled brownies.

OATMEAL DROP COOKIES
5 dozens

2 cups sifted all-purpose flour
1 teaspoon soda
1 teaspoon salt
1½ teaspoons cinnamon
2 cups quick-cooking oatmeal

1 cup soft shortening, butter or margarine (¾ cup for soft cookies)
½ cup granulated sugar
¾ cup brown sugar, firmly packed
2 eggs
1½ teaspoons vanilla
⅓ cup milk or buttermilk
1 cup raisins, chopped dates or chocolate chips
¾ cup chopped nuts, if desired

Preheat oven to 375° F. Sift together flour, soda, salt and cinnamon. Add oatmeal. Combine butter, sugars, eggs and vanilla in large Mixmaster Mixer bowl. Cream at No. 7 2 minutes. Stop Mixer and add milk, then flour mixture gradually while beating at No. 1 speed until blended. Add raisins and nuts. Beat at No. 4 speed for 1½ minutes. Drop by teaspoonfuls on greased cookie sheet. Bake about 12 minutes or until browned.

QUICK APPLE-GINGER BARS
40 bars

1 package gingerbread mix
1 can (8½ ounces) applesauce
½ cup raisins
1 jar (4 ounces) mixed candied fruits and peels
2 cups sifted confectioners sugar
Milk
1 teaspoon lemon juice
1 teaspoon grated lemon peel

Preheat oven to 375° F. Put gin-

Recipe books for new Blenders and Mixers contain information on speed settings for other models in front, Instruction Section.

145

gerbread mix and applesauce into large bowl of Mixmaster Mixer. With Dial set at No. 5, beat 2 minutes. Turn Dial to No. 1 and stir in raisins and peels. Spread in a greased 15½- by 10- by 1-inch jelly-roll pan and bake 15 to 20 minutes. Cool. Mix confectioners sugar with enough milk to make spreading consistency. Stir in lemon juice and peel. Spread thinly on baked gingerbread. Cut into bars.

LEMON MOONS
about 4 dozens

2 cups sifted all-purpose flour
2 teaspoons baking powder
½ teaspoon salt
¼ teaspoon mace
2 eggs
⅔ cup cooking oil
1 cup sugar, divided
¼ cup brown sugar
2 teaspoons grated lemon peel
2 teaspoons lemon juice
½ teaspoon nutmeg

Preheat oven to 400° F. Sift together flour, baking powder, salt and mace. Reserve. In large Mixmaster Mixer bowl combine eggs, oil, ¾ cup sugar, brown sugar, lemon peel and juice. With Dial set at No. 1, blend these ingredients. Set Dial at No. 5 and beat until thick. Return Dial to No. 1 and blend in dry ingredients. Drop by teaspoonfuls on greased cookie sheet. Combine nutmeg and remaining

sugar. Butter the bottom of a glass; dip in sugar mixture and press each cookie flat. Bake about 8 minutes.

STOVE-TOP CHOCOLATE SOUFFLE
4 servings

2 squares unsweetened chocolate
1 cup milk
½ cup sugar
⅛ teaspoon salt
1 teaspoon vanilla
3 eggs
Whipped cream

Combine chocolate, milk, sugar and salt in top part of a double boiler. Place over boiling water and heat until chocolate is melted. Beat with a Mixmaster Hand Mixer, or Mixmaster Mixer removed from stand, until mixture is smooth. Add vanilla and eggs while continuing to beat. Beat mixture 1 minute. Cover and cook 20 minutes. Serve hot or cold, with whipped cream.

CHILLY CHEESE
4 to 6 servings

1 cup cottage cheese
1 cup sour cream
½ cup confectioners sugar
1 teaspoon vanilla
Strawberry preserves

Put all ingredients except preserves into Sunbeam Blender.

Cover and process at Mix a few seconds. Spoon into individual dessert dishes and chill. Serve topped with preserves.

BAKED ALASKA
6 to 8 servings

1 quart ice cream, slightly softened
1 pint sherbet
8-inch yellow cake layer
5 egg whites
¾ cup sugar

Preheat oven to 450° F. Line 1½-quart mixing bowl with wax paper or aluminum foil. Pack slightly softened ice cream along bottom and sides of bowl. Fill center with sherbet. Place a piece of wax paper on top of ice cream and press flat. Freeze until firm. Cut out a double layer of heavy brown paper at least 1 inch larger than the cake layer. Place on a baking sheet, place cake layer on paper and chill in refrigerator. Place egg whites in large bowl of Mixmaster Mixer. Beat at No. 12 until egg whites form moist peaks. Slowly add sugar, 2 tablespoonfuls at a time, and continue beating until whites are stiff and glossy. Invert ice cream onto cake layer and peel off paper. Quickly cover ice cream and cake completely with meringue. At this point the whole Alaska can be

returned to freezer and kept until dessert time or it can be baked and served immediately. Bake 4 to 5 minutes or just until meringue is delicately browned. Transfer Alaska to chilled platter. Serve immediately.

LEMON SNOW
8 servings

1 envelope unflavored gelatin
½ cup sugar
¼ teaspoon salt
1 can (6 ounces) frozen lemonade, unthawed
2 egg whites
Whole fresh strawberries

Combine gelatin, sugar and salt in a small bowl. Add 1¼ cups hot water and stir until gelatin is dissolved. Add lemonade and blend well. Chill mixture in refrigerator until slightly thickened. Place bowl in a bowl of ice and water. Add unbeaten egg whites. Beat with Mixmaster Hand Mixer, or Mixmaster Mixer removed from stand, until mixture forms soft peaks. Pour into 1½-quart ring mold. Chill until firm. Unmold on a chilled serving plate and fill center with whole berries.

BURNT ALMOND SPONGE
8 servings

2 tablespoons unflavored gelatin
1½ cups sugar, divided

Recipe books for new Blenders and Mixers contain information on speed settings for other models in front, Instruction Section.

147

1¼ cups milk
½ teaspoon salt
1½ cups heavy cream, whipped
¾ cup slivered almonds,
    toasted
1 teaspoon vanilla

Sprinkle gelatin over ¾ cup cold water; allow to soften. Heat 1⅛ cups sugar in a heavy skillet. As sugar melts, stir until a rich brown. Scald the milk; add the sugar syrup gradually, stirring constantly. Remove from heat. Pour into large bowl of Mixmaster Mixer; add remaining sugar, softened gelatin and salt. Refrigerate until mixture begins to thicken and is jelly-like. Remove from refrigerator; with Dial set at No. 6, beat until spongy. With Dial set at No. 1, fold in whipped cream. Fold in almonds and vanilla. Pour into serving dish or dishes. Refrigerate until set.

ALMOND-ORANGE MOUSSE
8 servings

1 cup sugar
3 tablespoons grated orange
    rind
1 tablespoon unflavored gelatin
1 cup orange juice
¼ cup lemon juice
¾ cup heavy cream
1 cup slivered toasted almonds

Put sugar, orange rind and ½ cup boiling water in a small saucepan; boil 1 minute. Soften

gelatin in ¼ cup cold water. Dissolve in hot syrup. Add orange and lemon juice and refrigerate until mixture begins to thicken. Place cream in large bowl of Mixmaster Mixer; with Dial set at No. 9, whip until stiff. Turn Dial to No. 1 and fold in orange mixture; add almonds, fold just until blended in. Pour into serving dish or dishes. Refrigerate until set.

SUPERB CHOCOLATE MOUSSE
4 servings

1 package (6 ounces) semisweet
    chocolate bits
2 eggs
3 tablespoons strong, hot coffee
1 to 2 tablespoons rum, brandy,
    Curaçao or Grand Marnier
¾ cup milk, scalded

Combine all ingredients in Sunbeam Blender. Cover and process at Mix 2 minutes. Pour into 4 dessert dishes and refrigerate at least 4 hours.

SPIRITED CREAM
8 servings

½ cup cold milk
2 envelopes unflavored gelatin
½ cup hot milk
2 eggs
⅓ cup sugar

⅛ teaspoon salt
2 tablespoons coffee liqueur
or fruit liqueur
1 cup heavy cream
1½ cups crushed ice

Put cold milk and gelatin in Sunbeam Blender. Cover and process at Stir to soften gelatin. Remove Feeder Cap and add hot milk to dissolve gelatin. Process at Stir. If gelatin granules cling to container, use a rubber spatula to push them down. Add eggs, sugar, salt and liqueur. Process at Whip. Add cream and ice and continue to process at Liquefy until ice is liquefied. Pour into individual dishes or a 5-cup mold. Chill until firm.

CHOCOLATE RUM MOUSSE
8 servings

¼ cup cold milk
1 envelope unflavored gelatin
¾ cup milk, heated to boiling
6 tablespoons dark rum
1 egg
¼ cup sugar
⅛ teaspoon salt
1 package (6 ounces) semisweet chocolate pieces
1 cup heavy cream
2 ice cubes

Put cold milk and gelatin in Sunbeam Blender. Cover and process at Stir until gelatin is softened. Remove Feeder Cap and add hot milk. Blend at Stir until gelatin dissolves. If gelatin granules cling to sides of container, stop Blender and use a rubber spatula to push them down. When gelatin is dissolved add rum, egg, sugar, salt and chocolate pieces. Process at Beat until mixture is smooth. Add cream and ice cubes and process at Liquefy until ice is liquefied. Pour into parfait or wine glasses or a 1½-quart dessert dish. Chill until firm. Serve with whipped cream if desired.

CHERRY CHEESE PIE
6 to 8 servings

1 package (8 ounces) cream cheese
1 can (14 ounces) sweetened condensed milk
⅓ cup lemon juice
1 teaspoon vanilla
9-inch pie shell, baked
1 can (1 pound 4 ounces) cherry-pie filling

Put cream cheese in small bowl of Mixmaster Mixer. Beat at No. 2 speed until slightly softened. Add milk slowly and beat until blended. Add lemon juice and vanilla. Beat at No. 9 speed until mixture is smooth and very thick. Spoon mixture into pie shell. Top with cherry-pie filling. Chill before serving.

Recipe books for new Blenders and Mixers contain information on speed settings for other models in front, Instruction Section.

149

STRAWBERRY SOUFFLE
6 servings

1 pint strawberries
1¼ cups sugar, divided
1 envelope unflavored gelatin
4 eggs, separated
⅛ teaspoon salt
1 cup heavy cream, whipped

Fold a long strip of wax paper or aluminum foil so that it is about 4 inches wide and long enough to extend around the outside of a 1½-quart soufflé dish. Lightly brush one side of the strip with oil. Fasten the strip, oiled side in, around top of soufflé dish. It can be tied with string or clipped together with paper clips. Clean berries. Put in Sunbeam Blender and process at Puree. Pour berries into a 2-cup measure. There should be about 1⅓ cups purée. Stir ½ cup sugar into the berries. Remove ¼ cup of the purée. Sprinkle gelatin over top and let stand to soften. Combine egg yolks with ½ cup sugar in top of double boiler. Cook over boiling water, stirring until mixture is thickened. Add gelatin mixture and stir until gelatin is dissolved. Cool. Blend in remaining strawberry purée. Place egg whites and salt in large bowl of Mixmaster Mixer. Beat at No. 12 until foamy. Gradually add remaining ¼ cup sugar and continue beating until mixture is shiny and forms stiff peaks. Fold in whipped cream. Gently fold in strawberry mixture. Turn mixture into prepared soufflé dish. Chill until firm. Remove collar and serve.

SOUR CREAM PIE
6 to 8 servings

2 eggs
1 cup sour cream
1 cup seeded raisins
⅔ cup sugar
1½ teaspoons cinnamon
¼ teaspoon salt
¾ cup pecans
9-inch pastry shell, unbaked

Preheat oven to 450° F. Put first 6 ingredients into Sunbeam Blender; cover and process at Chop. When well mixed, turn off Blender and add pecans; chop briefly. Pour mixture into an unbaked pie shell. Bake 15 minutes; lower oven temperature to 350° and bake 30 minutes or until set.

CUSTARD PIE
4 to 6 servings

4 eggs
⅔ cup sugar
½ teaspoon salt
¼ teaspoon nutmeg

1 teaspoon vanilla
2 cups milk, scalded
8-inch pie shell, unbaked

Preheat oven to 350° F. Put eggs, sugar, salt, nutmeg and vanilla into Sunbeam Blender; cover and process at Whip until sugar is dissolved and eggs are lemon-colored. Remove Feeder Cap and add milk; continue to process until well blended. Pour into an unbaked pie shell. Bake for about 30 minutes until a silver knife inserted in the custard comes out clean.

CRUMB CRUST
9-inch shell

Graham crackers, cookies or
zwieback
2 tablespoons sugar
½ teaspoon cinnamon
⅓ cup melted butter or
margarine

Blender-crumb crackers in Sunbeam Blender. Empty into a measuring cup. Repeat the process until 1 cup crumbs is made. Empty into a bowl. Add sugar, cinnamon and melted butter. Mix thoroughly. Pat onto bottom and sides of a 9-inch pie pan. Chill before filling.

Serving style: Any cream filling —chocolate, vanilla, butterscotch—is delicious in this crust.

LEMON MIST CHEESE PIE
6 to 8 servings

3 eggs, separated
1½ cups creamed cottage cheese
⅔ cup light cream
3 tablespoons lemon juice
1 teaspoon grated lemon rind
⅔ cup sugar
1 tablespoon flour
¼ teaspoon salt
1 unbaked 9-inch pie shell

Preheat oven to 450° F. Put egg yolks in large bowl and egg whites in small bowl of Mixmaster Mixer. Turn Dial to No. 12 and beat egg whites until stiff but not dry. Set aside. With same beaters, beat egg yolks on No. 12. Add cottage cheese, cream, lemon juice, lemon rind and beat at No. 4 until thoroughly mixed. Add sugar, flour and salt, and continue to beat until well mixed. With Dial set at No. 1. fold into egg whites gently. Pour mixture into pie shell. Bake 10 minutes; reduce heat to 325° F. and bake 35 to 40 minutes or until a knife inserted in the center comes out clean.

FROZEN STRAWBERRY PIE
8 servings

Vanilla wafers
Walnuts or pecans

½ cup butter or margarine,
melted
1 package (10 ounces) frozen
sliced strawberries, thawed
½ cup sugar
1 egg white
1 cup sour cream

Preheat oven to 350° F. Break a few vanilla wafers into Sunbeam Blender. Process at Grate until of desired consistency. Pour crumbs into a measuring cup and continue process until 1½ cups crumbs are made. Blender-chop nuts to make ½ cup finely chopped nuts. Combine crumbs, nuts and butter and blend thoroughly. Press mixture firmly on bottom and sides of a 10-inch pie plate. Bake 10 minutes; cool. In large bowl of Mixmaster Mixer combine strawberries, sugar and egg white. Turn to No. 10 and beat until soft peaks form, about 10 minutes. Remove and fold in sour cream with a rubber spatula. Spoon into crust and place pie in freezer. When chilled, make swirls on top. Freeze until firm.

PECAN PIE
8 servings
2 eggs
¾ cup sugar
1 cup dark corn syrup
2 tablespoons melted butter
1 tablespoon flour

1 teaspoon vanilla
⅛ teaspoon salt
1 cup pecan halves
1 unbaked 9-inch pie crust

Preheat oven to 400° F. Place eggs in small bowl of Mixmaster Mixer. With Dial at No. 4, beat lightly. Add next 6 ingredients and beat at No. 2 until well blended. Stir in pecan halves and pour into pie crust. Bake 15 minutes; lower heat to 350° and bake 30 to 35 minutes longer until set. Cool before serving.

Serving style: A fluff of whipped cream makes this even better. Leave the cream unsweetened; the pie is sweet enough.

SOMETHING SPECIAL PUMPKIN PIE
6 to 8 servings

1 package (8 ounces) cream
cheese, softened
¾ cup brown sugar, firmly
packed
1 teaspoon cinnamon
1 teaspoon nutmeg
½ teaspoon ginger
½ teaspoon salt
3 eggs
1 cup canned pumpkin
1 cup milk
1 unbaked 9-inch pie shell
Whipped cream

Preheat oven to 375° F. Place cheese, sugar, spices and salt in large bowl of Mixmaster Mixer. With Dial set at No. 1, blend

Recipe books for new Blenders and Mixers contain information on speed settings for other models in front, Instruction Section.

153

ingredients; set Dial at No. 5 and beat 1 minute. Add eggs, 1 at a time; beat well after each addition. Turn Dial back to No. 1 and stir in pumpkin and milk. Pour into pie shell and bake 45 to 50 minutes. Serve chilled, with whipped cream.

STRAWBERRY TARTS
8 servings

*1 package (10 ounces) pie
crust mix
2 pints fresh strawberries
1 cup sugar
3 tablespoons cornstarch
1 pint heavy cream*

Preheat oven to 450° F. Prepare pie crust mix according to package directions. Roll out to ¼-inch thickness and cut into 8 4-inch circles. Fit each circle loosely into a custard cup. Prick well with a fork. Bake 10 to 15 minutes until browned. Wash and hull berries. Slice half of berries, reserving remainder. Divide sliced berries among cooled tart shells. Place remaining berries in Sunbeam Blender. Add ½ cup water and process at Puree until berries are puréed. Place puréed berries in a saucepan. Add sugar. Cook over low heat until sugar is dissolved. Dissolve cornstarch in 3 tablespoons water and add to saucepan. Cook, stirring constantly until smooth and thickened. Pour this sauce over sliced ber-

ries in tart shells. Chill until firm. At serving time, place cream in bowl and with Mixmaster Hand Mixer set at medium speed, whip until stiff. Top tarts with cream.

TWO-BERRY PIE
4 to 6 servings

*Graham crackers
⅓ cup sugar
⅓ cup soft butter or margarine
1 package (10 ounces) frozen
raspberries
1 teaspoon vanilla
1 pint fresh strawberries,
washed, hulled
½ cup heavy cream
2 tablespoons confectioners
sugar*

Break each cracker into several pieces. Place in Sunbeam Blender a few pieces at a time. Process at Grate until 1½ cups crumbs are obtained. Mix cracker crumbs, sugar, butter; press onto bottom and sides of a 9-inch pie plate. Chill. Combine raspberries and vanilla in Blender; cover and process at Puree until smooth. Pour purée into crumb crust. Set strawberries, point up, into purée. In small Mixmaster Mixer bowl whip cream until stiff with Dial set at No. 9. Sweeten with confectioners sugar. Top pie with whipped cream.

Index

Appetizers, Cold
Braunschweiger Spread, 8
Clam Dip, 9
Club Cheddar Dip, 8
Crab Meat Spread, 9
Egg and Avocado Dip, 10
Eggplant Dip, 13
Lobster Spread, 9
Party Pâté, 7
Pimiento Cheese Dip, 13
Quick Pâté, 14
Red Cheese Ball, 13
Roquefort Cheese Dip, 12
Seashore Dip, 7
Sherry Cheddar Cheese, 9
Shrimp Dip, 12
Shrimp Soup Dip, 8
South-of-the-Border Dip, 12
Swiss Cheese Dip, 12
Tantalizer Spread, 8
Appetizers, Hot
Appetizer Meatballs, 10
Cheese Puffs, 14
Fried Chicken Wings, 14
Stuffed Mushrooms, 10
Beverages, Alcoholic
Alexander, 85
Bacardi Cocktail, 86
Bloody Mary, 86
Coffee Cocktail, 85
Collins, 85
Daiquiri, 84
Eggnogg, 86
Grasshopper, 84
Orange Blossom, 85
Pink Lady, 86
Scarlett O'Hara, 85
Screwdriver, 86
Whiskey Sour, 84
Beverages, Nonalcoholic
Apri-Coffee Frost, 79
Breakfast in a Glass, 80
Candy Cane Punch, 81
Carrot-Pineapple Cocktail, 82
Chocolate Milk Shake, Malted, 84
Cold Eggnog, 79
Freshly Ground Coffee, 82
Hot Chocolate, 80
Lemon-Strawberry Punch, 80
Mexican Chocolate, 79
Mint Malt, 81
Peach Cooler, 81
Pineapple Mint Splash, 82
Pink Lassies, 82
Spicy Apple Eggnog, 80
Strawberry Smoothee, 79
Sunbeam Slimmer, 81
Tomato Juice Cocktail, 84
Beef
Barbecued Meat Loaf, 44
Barbecued Short Ribs, 33
Beef and Beer, 39
Beef Roulades, 39
Beef Roulades with Roquefort, 36
Boeuf Bourguignonne, 122
Braised Stuffed Flank Steak, 34
Broiled Steak, 42

Burger Stroganoff, 44
Burgundy Burgers, 42
Carpetbag Steak. 38
Cheesed Corned Beef Hash, 119
Chicken-Fried Steak, 39
Chipped Beef and Artichokes, 116
Citrus Swiss Steak, 38
Classic Beef Rolls, 123
Creole Liver, 46
Greek Macaroni Bake, 124
Hamburger Oriental Style, 41
Hungarian Goulash, 41
Hungarian Hunters' Stew, 37
Mandarin Beef, 125
Mushroom Wine Burgers, 45
Pepper Steak, 37
Porcupine Meatballs, 41
Pot Roast with Vegetables, 34
Quick Wine Steaks, 34
Rolled Flank Steaks, 123
Savory Steaks on Toast, 37
South Seas Beef, 42
Spaghetti with Meatballs, 45
Steak Diane, 33
Stuffed Teenburgers, 118
Sukiyaki, 127
Swedish Meatballs, 40
Teriyaki Pot Roast, 33
Breads, Other Baked Treats
Baking Powder Biscuits, 100
Bran Muffins, 103
Cheese Muffins, 99
Cranberry-Nut Loaf, 103
Doughnut Puffs, 108
Griddle Cakes, 106
Lemon Muffins, 108
Oatmeal Nut Bread, 101
Orange-Date Loaf, 101
Orange Pecan Waffles, 104
Peanut Butter Orange Bread, 104
Poori, 128
Popovers, 100
Quick Basic Muffins, 100
Scotch Cream Scones, 105
Spoon Bread, 100
Stovepipe Bread, 103
Sugary Spice Puffs, 106
Sunday Brunch Coffee Cake, 99
Waffles, 105
Cakes
Angel Food Cake, 138
Birthday Cake, 136
Cherry Cake, 136
Chocolate Fleck Cake, 136
Chocolate Fudge Cake, 137
Chocolate Marble Cake, 136
Chocolate-Nut Torte, 133
Coffee Cake with Streusel Topping, 136
Cupcakes, 136
Dressed-Up Cake Mixes, 135
French-Toasted Pound Cake, 113
Greek Nut Cake, 130
Jiffy One-Egg Cake, 136
Large Birthday Cake, 137
Lemon Cake, 135

Mocha Bundt Cake, 135
Orange-Plus Cake, 135
Pecan Log, 138
Silver Layer Cake, 135
Upside-Down Cake, 137

Chicken
Chicken Breasts Buffet Style, 60
Chicken Breasts with Mushrooms, 47
Chicken Cacciatore, 53
Chicken Encore, 58
Chicken Fricassee, 47
Chicken Hungarian, 53
Chicken Kiev, 55
Chicken Livers with Eggs, 117
Chicken Marengo, 55
Chicken Maximilian, 52
Chicken with Pea Pods, 49
Chicken Tarragon, 48
Chicken in White Wine, 48
Coq au Vin, 129
Country Captain, 57
Flaming Breast of Chicken, 56
Fried Chicken, 58
Frypan Stir-Fry Chicken, 114
Lemon Quick Chick, 48
Quick Chicken à la King, 50
Quick Chicken Stroganoff, 50
Stewed Chicken with Dumplings, 56
Trade Winds Chicken 49

Cookies
Brownies, 144
Lemon Moons, 146
Nut Macaroons, 144
Oatmeal Drop Cookies, 145
Old-Fashioned Soft Sugar Cookies, 144
Quick Apple-Ginger Bars, 145
Quick Chocolate Chip Cookies, 143
Spritz Cookies, 143

Desserts, Miscellaneous
Almond-Orange Mousse, 148
Baked Alaska, 147
Cherries Jubilee, 114
Cherry Waffle Sundaes, 113
Chilly Cheese, 146
Chocolate Rum Mousse, 149
Dessert Pancakes, 112
Iranian Pancakes, 132
Italian Cheesecake, 129
Marmalade Dessert Omelets, 113
Stove-Top Chocolate Soufflé, 146
Strawberry Cheesecake, 140
Strawberry Soufflé, 151
Superb Chocolate Mousse, 148
Swedish Fattigman, 143

Eggs
Brunch Eggs, 111
Brunch Omelet, 110
Creamy Chicken Omelet, 58
Farmers' Breakfast, 110
Italian Brunch, 110
Scrambled Eggs with Water Chestnuts, 111
Sunday Breakfast Eggs, 109
Swiss Eggs, 109

Fish and Shellfish
Almond Tomato Fillets, 65
Barbecued Fish Fillets, 63
Batter-Dipped Fish, 61
Breaded Fish Parmesan, 63
Chinese Supper, 70

Codfish Cakes, 64
Crab à la Dewey, 117
Crisp-Fried Fish, 62
Deviled Salmon, 65
Fillet of Sole Werner, 122
Fish Balls, 62
Fish Duglere, 68
French Fried Shrimp, 119
Fried Fish, 61
Fried Shrimp, 66
Lobster Cantonese, 69
Marinated Fish, 63
Party Crab Meat, 120
Poached Fish with Garlic Sauce, 121
Scallops Cacciatore, 64
Scampi, 68
Seafood au Gratin, 116
Seafood Méditerranée, 66
Seaside Loaf, 70
Shrimp Bahama, 118
Shrimp Buffet Casserole, 65
Shrimp Mousse Elégante, 62
Sole Belle Aurore, 69
Sole in Mousseline Sauce, 68

Frostings
Basic Uncooked Butter Frosting, 141
Chocolate Frosting, 143
Fluffy Frosting, 141
Lady Baltimore Frosting, 141
Lemon or Orange Frosting, 141
Maple Frosting, 141
Mocha Frosting, 141
Sea Foam Frosting, 141
Strawberry Frosting, 141

Lamb
Cranberry Shoulder Lamb Chops, 31
Irish Stew, 30
Lamb Shoulder Chops, Pizza Style, 32
Leg of Lamb with White Beans, 30
Mandarin Lamb Shanks, 32
Savory Lamb Chops, 32
Sherried Lamb Chops, 31
Spanish Lamb Stew, 27

Pies and Pastries
Cherry Cheese Pie, 149
Crumb Crust, 152
Custard Pie, 151
Frozen Strawberry Pie, 152
Lemon Mist Cheese Pie, 152
Pecan Pie, 153
Something Special Pumpkin Pie, 153
Sour Cream Pie, 151
Strawberry Tarts, 154
Two-Berry Pie, 154

Pork
Barbecued Pork Chops, 25
French-Toasted Hamwiches, 119
Gourmet Pork Chops, 23
Paprika Ham, 25
Pork and Cabbage Skillet, 24
Pork and Sauerkraut, 26
Pork Chops in Vermouth, 23
Pork Tenderloin in Cream, 25
Sauerkraut Skillet, 26
Sweet and Sour Pork, 24

Puddings
Burnt Almond Sponge, 147
Cold Wine Custard, 130
Golden Clouds, 132
Lemon Snow, 147
Spirited Cream, 148

Salad Dressings
Anchovy Dressing, 95
Apricot-Honey Dressing, 96
Avocado Dressing, 96
Basic French Dressing, 95
Blender Mayonnaise, 93
Blue Cheese or Roquefort Dressing, 93
Celery Seed Dressing, 95
Creamy Garlic Dressing, 93
Fruit Dressing, 92
Imperial Valley Blue Cheese
    Dressing, 92
Lime Honey Fruit Dressing, 95
Low Calorie Dressing, 96
Old-Fashioned Salad Dressing, 93
Thousand Island Dressing, 96
Salads
Baked Chicken Salad, 87
Balkan Cucumbers, 90
Celery Remoulade, 89
Cranberry Dream Salad, 92
Cranberry Mold, 89
Cucumber Mousse, 90
Frozen Peach-Pecan Salad, 91
Herbed Chicken and Olive Mousse, 88
Hot German Potato Salad, 91
Lime-Cheese Salad, 91
Mideastern Chicken Salad, 87
Peach-Almond Soufflé Salad, 88
Salad of Gold, 89
Strassburg Salad, 88
Sauces
Béarnaise Sauce, 98
Fresh Horseradish Sauce, 98
Italian Tomato Sauce, 128
Lemon Parsley Sauce, 98
Quick Hollandaise Sauce, 97
Sauce Elégante, 62
Sauce Verte, 98
Spaghetti Sauce, 45
Sweet-Sour Basting Sauce, 97
Western Barbecue Sauce, 97
Soups, Cold
Borscht, 16
Frosty Sour-Cream Tomato Soup, 18
Gazpacho, 17
Springtime Pea Soup, 20
Superb Asparagus Soup, 17
Vichyssoise, 18

Soups, Hot
Beef Vegetable Soup, 15
Chicken Gumbo Soup, 21
Cream of Carrot Soup, 15
Cream of Celery Soup, 18
Cream of Mushroom Soup, 16
Curried Pea Soup, 16
Mexican Meatball Soup, 20
Onion Soup, 21
Split Pea Soup, 21
Summer Tomato Soup, 22
Supreme Tomato Soup, 17
Tuna Bisque, 16
Tuna Chowder, 20
Turkey
Sweet and Pungent Turkey, 52
Turkey Breast Marsala, 117
Veal
Braised Shoulder of Veal, 29
Glorious Liver, 46
Party Veal Rolls, 28
Lemon Veal Stew, 27
Osso Buco Milanese Style, 26
Veal Chops with Mushrooms, 29
Veal in Cream, 125
Veal Italienne, 28
Vegetables and Side Dishes
Baked Carrot Puffs, 78
Candied Sweet Potatoes, 72
Cheese Potato Patties, 74
Corn Pudding, 71
French Fried Onions, 72
French Fried Potatoes, 73
Fried Cheese, 77
Golden Onions, 71
Indian Summer Vegetables, 76
Italian Eggplant Parmigiana, 127
Italian Rice Balls, 112
Mashed Potatoes, 74
Oriental-Style Broccoli, 76
Pennsylvania Red Cabbage, 72
Potato Pancakes, 78
Potato Puffs, 71
Sautéed Carrots, 120
Sautéed Mushrooms, 72
Sautéed Onions, 74
Skillet Zucchini, 77
Special Carrots, 77
Stuffed Tomatoes, 74

Index of Recipes by Appliance

Mixmaster Hand Mixer
Brunch Omelet, 110
Chicken Kiev, 55
Fluffy Frosting, 141
French-Toasted Hamwiches, 119
French-Toasted Pound Cake, 113
Greek Nut Cake, 130
Italian Brunch, 110
Lemon Snow, 147
Quick Hollandaise Sauce, 97
Quick Pate, 14
Rolled Flank Steak, 123
Scrambled Eggs with Water
    Chestnuts, 111
Sole in Mousseline Sauce, 68
Spicy Apple Eggnog, 80

Stove-Top Chocolate Soufflé, 146
Strawberry Tarts, 154
Mixmaster Mixer
Almond-Orange Mousse, 148
Angel Food Cake, 137
Baked Alaska, 147
Baked Carrot Puffs, 77
Baking Powder Biscuits, 100
Balkan Cucumbers, 90
Barbecued Meat Loaf, 44
Basic Uncooked Butter Frosting, 141
Batter-Dipped Fish, 61
Birthday Cake, 136
Bran Muffins, 103
Brownies, 144
Burnt Almond Sponge, 147
Celery Remoulade, 89

Cheese Muffins, 99
Cheese Puffs, 14
Cherry Cake, 136
Cherry Cheese Pie, 149
Chocolate Fudge Cake, 137
Chocolate Fleck Cake, 136
Chocolate Marble Cake, 136
Chocolate-Nut Torte, 133
Codfish Cakes, 64
Cold Wine Custard, 130
Cranberry-Nut Loaf, 103
Creamy Chicken Omelet, 58
Custard Topping, 124
Dessert Pancakes, 112
Doughnut Puffs, 108
Dressed-Up Cake Mixes
  Lemon, 135
  Mocha Bundt, 135
  Orange-Plus, 135
Eggplant Dip, 13
Fluffy Frosting, 141
  Sea Foam, 141
  Lady Baltimore, 141
Fried Shrimp, 66
Frozen Strawberry Pie, 152
Golden Clouds, 132
Greek Nut Cake, 130
Griddle Cakes, 106
Italian Cheesecake, 129
Iranian Pancakes, 132
Jiffy One-Egg Cake, 136
  Cupcakes, 136
  Coffee, with Streusel Topping, 136
  Upside-Down, 137
Large Birthday Cake, 137
Lemon Mist Cheese Pie, 152
Lemon Moons, 146
Lemon Muffins, 108
Lemon Snow, 147
Marmalade Dessert Omelets, 113
Mashed Potatoes, 74
Nut Macaroons, 144
Oatmeal Drop Cookies, 145
Old-Fashioned Salad Dressing, 93
Old-Fashioned Soft Sugar Cookies, 144
Orange-Date Loaf, 101
Orange Pecan Waffles, 104
Peach-Almond Soufflé Salad, 88
Peanut Butter Orange Bread, 104
Pecan Log, 138
Pecan Pie, 153
Quick Apple-Ginger Bars, 145
Quick Basic Muffins, 100
Quick Chocolate Chip Cookies, 143
Quick Hollandaise Sauce, 97
Quick Pâté, 14
Scotch Cream Scones, 105
Silver Layer Cake, 135
Something Special Pumpkin Pie, 153
Spoon Bread, 100
Spritz Cookies, 143
Stovepipe Bread, 103
Stove-Top Chocolate Soufflé, 146
Strawberry Cheesecake, 140
Strawberry Soufflé, 151
Sugary Spice Puffs, 106
Sunday Breakfast Eggs, 109

Sunday Brunch Coffee Cake, 99
Swedish Fattigman, 143
Two-Berry Pie, 154
Waffles, 105

Multi-Cooker Frypan
Almond Tomato Fillets, 65
Appetizer Meatballs, 10
Barbecued Fish Fillets, 63
Barbecued Pork Chops, 25
Beef Roulades, 39
Beef Roulades with Roquefort, 36
Braised Stuffed Flank Steak, 34
Brunch Eggs, 111
Brunch Omelet, 110
Burger Stroganoff, 44
Burgundy Burgers, 42
Candied Sweet Potatoes, 72
Carpetbag Steak, 38
Cheesed Corned Beef Hash, 119
Cheese Potato Patties, 74
Cherries Jubilee, 114
Cherry Waffle Sundaes, 113
Chicken Breasts Buffet Style, 60
Chicken Breasts with Mushrooms, 47
Chicken Cacciatore, 53
Chicken Fricassee, 47
Chicken-Fried Steak, 39
Chicken Hungarian, 53
Chicken in White Wine, 48
Chicken Livers with Eggs, 117
Chicken Marengo, 55
Chicken Maximilian, 52
Chicken Tarragon, 48
Chicken with Pea Pods, 49
Chinese Supper, 70
Chipped Beef and Artichokes, 116
Classic Beef Rolls, 123
Country Captain, 57
Crab à la Dewey, 117
Cranberry Shoulder Lamb Chops, 31
Creole Liver, 46
Dessert Pancakes, 112
Farmers' Breakfast, 110
Fillet of Sole Werner, 122
Fish Duglere, 68
Flaming Breast of Chicken, 56
French-Toasted Hamwiches, 119
French-Toasted Pound Cake, 113
Fried Cheese, 77
Frypan Stir-Fry Chicken, 114
Glorious Liver, 46
Golden Onions, 71
Gourmet Pork Chops, 23
Greek Macaroni Bake, 124
Griddle Cakes, 106
Hamburger Oriental Style, 41
Hot German Potato Salad, 91
Hungarian Goulash, 41
Indian Summer Vegetables, 76
Iranian Pancakes, 132
Italian Brunch, 110
Italian Eggplant Parmigiana, 127
Lamb Shoulder Chops, Pizza Style, 32
Leg of Lamb with White Beans, 30
Lemon Quick Chick, 48
Lemon Veal Stew, 27
Lobster Cantonese, 69

Mandarin Beef, 125
Mandarin Lamb Shanks, 32
Marmalade Dessert Omelets, 113
Mushroom Wine Burgers, 45
Oriental-Style Broccoli, 76
Osso Buco Milanese Style, 26
Paprika Ham, 25
Party Crab Meat, 120
Party Veal Rolls, 28
Pepper Steak, 37
Poached Fish with Garlic Sauce, 121
Porcupine Meatballs, 41
Pork and Cabbage Skillet, 24
Pork Chops in Vermouth, 23
Pork Tenderloin in Cream, 25
Quick Chicken à la King, 50
Quick Chicken Stroganoff, 50
Quick Wine Steaks, 34
Rolled Flank Steak, 123
Sauerkraut Skillet, 26
Sautéed Carrots, 120
Sautéed Mushrooms, 72
Sautéed Onions, 74
Savory Lamb Chops, 31
Savory Steaks on Toast, 37
Scallops Cacciatore, 64
Scampi, 68
Scrambled Eggs with Water
    Chestnuts, 111
Seafood au Gratin, 116
Sherried Lamb Chops, 31
Shrimp Bahama, 118
Shrimp Buffet Casserole, 65
Skillet Zucchini, 77
Sole Belle Aurore, 69
Sole in Mousseline Sauce, 68
South Seas Beef, 42
Spaghetti with Meatballs, 45
Special Carrots, 77
Steak Diane, 33
Stuffed Mushrooms, 10
Stuffed Teenburgers, 118
Sukiyaki, 127
Sunday Breakfast Eggs, 109
Swedish Meatballs, 40
Sweet and Pungent Turkey, 52
Sweet and Sour Pork, 24
Swiss Eggs, 109
Trade Winds Chicken, 49
Turkey Breast Marsala, 117
Veal Chops with Mushrooms, 29
Veal in Cream, 125
Veal Italienne, 28
Sunbeam Blender
Alexander, 85
Anchovy Dressing, 95
Apri-Coffee Frost, 79
Apricot-Honey Dressing, 96
Avocado Dressing, 96
Bacardi Cocktail, 86
Baked Carrot Puffs, 78
Baked Chicken Salad, 87
Barbecued Meat Loaf, 44
Barbecued Pork Chops, 25
Basic French Dressing, 95
Béarnaise Sauce, 98
Blender Mayonnaise, 93

Bloody Mary, 86
Blue Cheese or Roquefort Dressing, 93
Borscht, 16
Braised Stuffed Flank Steak, 34
Bran Muffins, 103
Braunschweiger Spread, 8
Breakfast in a Glass, 80
Candy Cane Punch, 81
Carrot-Pineapple Cocktail, 82
Celery Seed Dressing, 95
Cheese Muffins, 99
Chicken Encore, 58
Chilly Cheese, 146
Chocolate Rum Mousse, 149
Chocolate Milk Shake, Malted, 84
Clam Dip, 9
Club Cheddar Dip, 8
Coffee Cocktail, 85
Cold Eggnog, 79
Collins, 85
Corn Pudding, 71
Crab Meat Spread, 9
Cranberry Dream Salad, 92
Cranberry Mold, 89
Cranberry-Nut Loaf, 103
Cranberry Shoulder Lamb Chops, 31
Cream of Carrot Soup, 15
Cream of Celery Soup, 18
Cream of Mushroom Soup, 16
Creamy Garlic Dressing, 93
Crumb Crust, 152
Cucumber Mousse, 90
Curried Pea Soup, 16
Custard Pie, 151
Daiquiri, 84
Deviled Salmon, 65
Egg and Avocado Dip, 10
Eggnog, 86
Fresh Horseradish Sauce, 98
Freshly Ground Coffee, 82
Frosty Sour-Cream Tomato Soup, 18
Frozen Peach-Pecan Salad, 91
Frozen Strawberry Pie, 152
Fruit Dressing, 92
Gazpacho, 17
Grasshopper, 84
Greek Nut Cake, 130
Herbed Chicken and Olive Mousse, 88
Hot Chocolate, 80
Imperial Valley Blue Cheese
    Dressing, 92
Italian Tomato Sauce, 128
Lemon Parsley Sauce, 98
Lemon-Strawberry Punch, 80
Lime-Cheese Salad, 91
Lime Honey Fruit Dressing, 95
Lobster Spread, 9
Low Calorie Dressing, 96
Mexican Chocolate, 79
Mideastern Chicken Salad, 87
Mint Malt, 81
Oatmeal Nut Bread, 101
Orange Blossom, 85
Orange-Date Loaf, 101
Party Pâté, 7
Peach Cooler, 81
Pecan Log, 138

Pennsylvania Red Cabbage, 72
Pimiento Cheese Dip, 13
Pineapple Mint Splash, 82
Pink Lady, 86
Pink Lassies, 82
Poached Fish with Garlic Sauce, 121
Popovers, 100
Potato Pancakes, 78
Red Cheese Ball, 13
Roquefort Cheese Dip, 12
Salad of Gold, 89
Sauce Elégante, 62
Sauce Verte, 98
Scallops Cacciatore, 64
Scarlett O'Hara, 85
Screwdriver, 86
Seashore Dip, 7
Seaside Loaf, 70
Sherry Cheddar Cheese, 9
Shrimp Dip, 12
Shrimp Mousse Elégante, 62
Shrimp Soup Dip, 8
Sole in Mousseline Sauce, 68
Sour Cream Pie, 151
South-of-the-Border Dip, 12
Spicy Apple Eggnog, 80
Spirited Cream, 148
Split Pea Soup, 21
Springtime Pea Soup, 20
Strassburg Salad, 88
Strawberry Cheesecake, 140
Strawberry Glaze, 140
Strawberry Smoothee, 79
Strawberry Soufflé, 151
Strawberry Tarts, 154
Stuffed Tomatoes, 74
Summer Tomato Soup, 22
Sunbeam Slimmer, 81
Superb Asparagus Soup, 17
Superb Chocolate Mousse, 147
Supreme Tomato Soup, 17
Sweet-Sour Basting Sauce, 97
Swiss Cheese Dip, 12
Tantalizer Spread, 8
Thousand Island Dressing, 96
Tomato Juice Cocktail, 84
Tuna Bisque, 16
Tuna Chowder, 20
Two-Berry Pie, 154
Vichyssoise, 18
Western Barbecue Sauce, 97
Whiskey Sour, 84

Sunbeam Cooker and Deep Fryer
Barbecued Short Ribs, 33
Batter-Dipped Fish, 61
Beef and Beer, 39
Beef Vegetable Soup, 15
Boeuf Bourguignonne, 122
Braised Shoulder of Veal, 29
Breaded Fish Parmesan, 63
Cheese Puffs, 14
Chicken Gumbo Soup, 21
Chicken Kiev, 55
Citrus Swiss Steak, 38
Codfish Cakes, 64
Coq au Vin, 129

Crisp-Fried Fish, 62
Doughnut Puffs, 108
Fish Balls, 62
French Fried Onions, 72
French Fried Potatoes, 73
French Fried Shrimp, 119
Fried Chicken, 58
Fried Chicken Wings, 14
Fried Fish, 61
Fried Shrimp, 66
Hungarian Hunters' Stew, 37
Irish Stew, 30
Italian Rice Balls, 112
Italian Tomato Sauce, 128
Leg of Lamb with White Beans, 30
Lemon Veal Stew, 27
Marinated Fish, 63
Mexican Meatball Soup, 20
Onion Soup, 21
Poori, 128
Pork and Sauerkraut, 26
Potato Puffs, 71
Pot Roast with Vegetables, 34
Rolled Flank Steak, 123
Seafood Méditerranée, 66
Spaghetti Sauce, 45
Spanish Lamb Stew, 27
Split Pea Soup, 21
Stewed Chicken with Dumplings, 56
Summer Tomato Soup, 22
Swedish Fattigman, 143
Sweet and Pungent Turkey, 52
Teriyaki Pot Roast, 33

Sunbeam Griddle
Dessert Pancakes, 112
Griddle Cakes, 106
Iranian Pancakes, 132
Potato Pancakes, 78
Scotch Cream Scones, 105

Sunbeam Knife
Beef and Beer, 39
Chicken with Pea Pods, 49
Frypan Stir-Fry Chicken, 114
Lemon Quick Chick, 48
Oriental-Style Broccoli, 76
Pork and Cabbage Skillet, 24
Pork Tenderloin in Cream, 25
Quick Chicken à la King, 50
Quick Chicken Stroganoff, 50
Sweet and Sour Pork, 24
Trade Winds Chicken, 49
Veal in Cream, 125

Sunbeam Broiler-Cover Frypan
Broiled Steak, 42

Sunbeam Toaster
Chicken Livers with Eggs, 117
Chipped Beef and Artichokes, 116
Crab à la Dewey, 117
Mushroom Wine Burgers, 45
Savory Steaks on Toast, 37
Seafood au Gatin, 116
Swiss Eggs, 109

Sunbeam Waffle Baker and Grill
Cherry Waffle Sundaes, 113
Orange Pecan Waffles, 104
Quick Chicken à la King, 50
Waffles, 105